Bird-Friendly Gardening

Quarto.com

© 2024 Quarto Publishing Group USA Inc.

Text © 2024 Jennifer McGuinness

First Published in 2024 by Cool Springs Press, an imprint of The Quarto Group,
100 Cummings Center, Suite 265-D, Beverly, MA 01915, USA.
T (978) 282-9590 F (978) 283-2742

Cool Springs Press titles are also available at discount for retail, wholesale, promotional, and bulk purchase. For details, contact the Special Sales Manager by email at specialsales@quarto.com or by mail at The Quarto Group, Attn: Special Sales Manager, 100 Cummings Center, Suite 265-D, Beverly, MA 01915, USA.

28 27 26 25 24 1 2 3 4 5

ISBN: 978-0-7603-8211-0

Digital edition published in 2024

eISBN: 978-0-7603-8212-7

Library of Congress Cataloging-in-Publication Data

Names: McGuinness, Jennifer, author.

Title: Bird-friendly gardening : guidance and projects for supporting birds in your landscape/Jennifer McGuinness.

Other titles: Guidance and projects for supporting birds in your landscape

Description: Beverly, MA, USA : Cool Springs Press, 2024. | Includes bibliographical references and index. | Summary: Bird-Friendly Gardening is the only book from this authoritative source on how to grow a living landscape that will welcome and support backyard birds—Provided by publisher.
Identifiers: LCCN 2023014432 | ISBN 9780760382110 (trade paperback) | ISBN 9780760382127 (ebook)
Subjects: LCSH: Gardening to attract birds—North America. | Bird attracting—North America. | Handbooks and manuals.
Classification: LCC QL676.55 .N38 2023 | DDC 598.072/34--dc23/eng/20230406
LC record available at https://lccn.loc.gov/2023014432

Design, page layout: Mattie Wells
Cover, large: Gray Catbird. Photo: Jen McGuinness
Cover, top: Western Tanager. Photo: Judd Patterson Photography
Cover, middle: Lazuli Bunting. Photo: Mia McPherson, On the Wing Photography
Cover, bottom: Northern Parula. Photo: Jen McGuinness
Back cover: Ruby-throated Hummingbird, Eastern Red Cedar, Northern Mockingbird, Purple Cone Flower, House Finch.
  Photos: Jen McGuinness
Illustration: Mattie Wells, Michael Wells

Printed in China

A Note About Bird Names

As this book went to press, the American Ornithological Society announced a new endeavor to rename certain bird species, in particular those named after people. At the time of publication, all of the names in this book were correct; however, by the time you read this book, some bird names featured in its pages may have changed. We will correct all changed names in future printings.

Bird-Friendly Gardening

Guidance and Projects for
Supporting Birds in Your Landscape

Jen McGuinness

COOL
SPRINGS
PRESS

Contents

Part III

BIRD-FRIENDLY GARDEN PROJECTS / 35

Part IV

CONCLUSION / 178

PART I

Introduction

Do you remember your "spark bird"—the one who piqued your interest in birdwatching or bird feeding?

For some, it's the brilliant red feathers of the Northern Cardinal. Or the determined, speedy flight of a Rufous Hummingbird. Or maybe it's a species so rare to see that you can only visit a bird sanctuary or aviary to get a glimpse of it in person.

Birds are marvels in their own right. Many migrate and travel vast distances in order to find food and a mate, and breed the next generation. They inhabit and adapt to our modern cities and suburban yards. But it's not easy. Every day more habitat that birds need to survive—either to provide food to eat, fresh water to drink, or trees and shrubs to seek cover and nest in—is destroyed. New paved parking lots, condos, expanded soccer fields—while it may not seem like a lot of space was removed in your own community, multiply it across the continental United States and that's a lot of land that has been whittled away.

In fact, there has been a 29 percent decrease in birds since 1970—that's a loss of 3 billion birds. There are 70 bird species that have lost two-thirds of their populations in the past 50 years—and are on track to lose another 50 percent in the next 50 years in North America (The State of the Birds Report 2022).

Combine that with the many exotic plants that are available at plant nurseries—which are valued and promoted because of the way they look in a landscape design. They are often not sources

A Prairie Warbler forages for insects in shrubby habitats.

of food for native insects and caterpillars, which means they do not provide food for songbirds.

Plants can offer so much more than a pleasant view in the garden. Lots of native plants have co-evolved with the surrounding area to support insects and birds. The best part is that many are easy to include in your garden.

Many bird admirers get started birdwatching or helping birds by adding bird feeders to their outdoor spaces, which is a great first step. But this is only one of the many ways you can make a difference for birds. Your private property can offer much more sustenance for songbirds than just sunflower seed in a hopper feeder. Using your garden, front yard, median strip, and even apartment balcony to create pockets of habitats that provide food, cover, and water can positively impact birds year-round.

This book will offer ideas to get you started on your journey. You'll read about individuals who have modified their property to make it hospitable for birds. No matter what your property size is—

small, medium, or large—there is a garden project that can be modified for your specific region. Adding native plants to your container gardens and outdoor areas and eliminating pesticide use, can offer a necessary respite for birds local to your area—and those who call it a temporary home during the migration season.

There's no better time than now to get started. The National Audubon Society estimates that 389 North American bird species are seriously threatened by climate change. Some of those birds include ones you may already see and can identify, such as the Baltimore Oriole, the Allen's Hummingbird, and several species of warblers. By making your property bird-friendly, you'll help ensure that we won't have to only visit bird sanctuaries or aviaries in the future to see the birds that coexist with us today.

NO MATTER WHERE YOU LIVE, THERE IS A WAY FOR YOU TO POSITIVELY IMPACT BIRDS

Birds have long held people's fascination—whether it is due to their colorful plumage, their ability to fly or their melodious song. There are more than 1,100 species of birds in the United States and Canada,

A Palm Warbler seeks insects along a wildlife preserve trail. In winter, this warbler does much of its foraging by walking and hopping on the ground.

and not surprisingly, birdwatching has continued to grow in popularity over the last several years.

In 2016, the U.S. Fish and Wildlife Service (USFWS) shared that 45 million Americans (age 16 and older) reported that they regularly observe birds—with 38.7 million people saying that activity takes place around their home. The National Audubon Society has attributed that 9 million of the 45 million Americans who are into birding are between the ages of 18 and 35 (as reported in a 2018 *New York Times* story).

This 9 million—also sharing an interest in birding and environmentalism activism—are a diverse group: 25 percent are Hispanic, 18 percent are African American, and 10 percent are Asian American (Green 2018).

Interestingly enough, these statistics were all taken before the 2020 COVID-19 pandemic, when social distancing and solo activities rose in popularity. Whether through a group outing or solo excursion, observing birds can often provide a necessary respite from the hustle and bustle of busy schedules. It's also accommodating to individuals of all skill levels, backgrounds, and physical abilities. Groups such as Birdability® focus on making outdoor areas inclusive, safe, and accessible to everyone, and events such as Black Birders Week aim to increase the visibility of this demographic group amongst birders and nature lovers.

Birdwatching is getting more tech savvy as well—the availability of apps on cell phones has provided an additional source of information for bird identification (using artificial intelligence to help ID birds through photos and sound) and list tracking.

Up your bird identification skills by downloading the Merlin Bird ID. The Sound ID feature listens to birds around you and suggests which birds may be singing in real-time. Or upload a photo of a bird seen in your garden and the Photo ID will offer possible matches to help you identify what you saw.

Social media also continues to be a way for bird enthusiasts to reach each other in order to share the excitement of bird sightings and learning.

Technology is also serving as an opportunity to find out more about birds' positive influences on humans. A 2022 study aimed to dig deeper into the connection with birding and mental health by asking participants to log their mood several times a day with a smartphone app whether they could see or hear birds or not. The study found that participants' mental well-being was significantly better when seeing or hearing birds compared to when not seeing or hearing birds. This positive effect of seeing or hearing birds on mental well-being increased when the individuals were outdoors, and was found to be beneficial to people with depression and people without a mental health condition (Hammoud, Tognin, Burgess, et al. 2022).

Other studies have also shown the positive influences of being out in nature. The best part—even though birdwatching is a popular activity, you don't need to travel far to see or hear birds. You can help them close to home.

Bird-friendly gardening is not a radical shift from gardening. In fact, you may already be doing it.

As mentioned earlier, native plants do a far better job of sustaining insect and bird life than exotic non-native plants. Many of the insects that birds use to rear their young are caterpillars. About 90 percent of the insects that eat plants can develop on only one or two plant lineages (Tallamy 2015). Omission of that plant removes the food source for birds. And 96 percent of songbirds feed insects to their young (Sorenson 2018).

When giving lectures about the importance of making private property more wildlife and insect friendly, entomologist Doug Tallamy often shares how many caterpillars are needed to raise one family of Black-capped Chickadees. It's between 6,000-7,000. Now think about all the other birds

Downy Woodpecker clings to a shepherd's hook pole in a garden.

in your neighborhood and in your state. Where will that food come from?

Lifelong gardeners may find a new appreciation for the species of plants that surround their homes, apartments, condos, and communities in providing not only visual interest and beauty but function and purpose. Native species in particular play an important role in the survival of songbirds that reside year-long in the garden and for those passing through during migration.

Layered gardens, which can be eye-catching and examples of great garden design, can also welcome a variety of birds that are drawn to the various layers either to forage or nest. Roughly described as the lower, mid, and tall levels, each level of plant life is filled with either individual plant species, shrubs, and low- or tall-growing trees.

In addition to selecting plants that are beneficial for birds—that will provide cover from predators, food throughout the seasons, and sometimes nesting material—bird-friendly gardening includes the following practices:

- Incorporating organic gardening with no pesticides or herbicides
- Leaving stems and seedheads
- Making brush piles for birds to hunt and hide in
- Leaving fallen leaves on your property
- Providing fresh water access

The importance of birds throughout history

The bird enthusiasts of today share a trait with the bird admirers of year's past—they are excited by birds! Birds have found a way to constantly fascinate people for a variety of reasons. Here are some examples:

- In ancient Egypt, the god Horus took the form of a falcon, and was considered one of the most important sky gods, who was associated with both the sun and the moon and protected royalty.

- In Native American culture, various birds were seen as good luck totems, such as the hummingbird, the woodpecker, and the flicker. The woodpecker was thought to bring wealth and both the woodpecker and flicker were thought to also bring happiness and healing. Small birds, such as wrens, chickadees, and swallows, were seen as messengers from the spirit world, and people were encouraged to feed them to keep them around the home (Lake-Thom 1997).

- Native Americans were also the first people to attract Purple Martins to artificial nesting structures by hanging dried gourds from trees near villages to encourage the birds to eat nuisance insects (Kress 2006).

- Before calendars were commonplace, Europeans used the arrival of the cuckoo to determine when to begin the farming season, since it reliably returned within the same time period each spring (Tate 2007).

- Passed down through history is the story that King Charles II (who reigned from 1660-1685) believed a prophecy that said England would fall if the six resident ravens left the Tower of London. Today, there are nine ravens in residence.

- In World War II, British Armed Forces relied on homing pigeons to deliver important messages during the war. Some were even awarded medals for bravery.

- Birds are also a major part of pop culture. Cartoon characters such as Tweety Bird, Woodstock, and Woody Woodpecker had starring roles in several cartoon series. Big Bird is a famous cast member of *Sesame Street*, who helps preschool children learn simple math and letter association. For older kids and adult fans of the wizarding world, Hedwig is the beloved Snowy Owl in the Harry Potter books. Many professional sports teams in North America use bird names to represent their teams (such as the Philadelphia Eagles, Atlanta Hawks, Pittsburgh Penguins, and Baltimore Orioles).

- Birds have even found their way into several proverbs and sayings, such as "the early bird gets the worm" to encourage good behavior and hard work. There's also "a bird in the hand is worth two in the bush," implying that it is better to hold onto something one has than to risk losing it by trying to get something better.

- In today's modern world, certain birds have retained symbolic meanings. Bluebirds symbolize happiness. Cardinals have been associated with angels or loved ones who have passed away. The Bald Eagle is synonymous with freedom and America. Doves are often associated with peace.

A Ruby-throated Hummingbird stands watch and guards a nearby nectar feeder.

- Keeping cats indoors
- Incorporating decals to warn birds of reflective surfaces

Bird enthusiasts can visit a variety of locations to view birds—especially during the spring and fall migration—but there is a thrill to having them come to your garden because of the choices you made to bring them. Why not make your outdoor spaces—whether it's a balcony, porch, or larger yard—more inviting to birds as well?

Attracting birds to a garden by providing supplemental food (seed, suet, or nectar) is common when most "natural food" is scarce or in short supply. But putting up feeders is only one way to support songbird populations. To attract the most diversity of birds, grow native plants. In fact, native plants—which provide either the insects, seeds, or berries that birds need to thrive—will feed a wider variety of birds than bird feeders alone.

Recalling the earlier mentioned 2016 USFWS survey, of the "wildlife watchers" who spend the majority of their time at home (also watching mammals, reptiles, insects, or fish), 69 percent feed wildlife, 35 percent photograph them, and 13 percent maintain plantings and natural areas to benefit wildlife. For natural areas that are maintained, 66 percent are on an acre or less of land, and 23 percent maintain 2 to 10 acres.

We often choose flowers and plants for their desired look in our landscape. But in some cases, it's not the bright blooms that bring the songbirds in—it's the spent blooms as they turn into seedheads.

Adding native plants to your garden or container plantings can happen gradually over time or all at once, depending on your available open space and exuberance. Adding native plants to your existing landscape—even if it currently includes non-native plants—will begin to offer more options to feed the birds in your area. Native plants, once established, also use less water, which can also help with cost-savings for water bills—whether in a container garden, back yard, or other spaces.

A Gray Catbird winters in the southern United States or the tropics, and travels north during the summer to breed.

The best part—you do not need to be an ornithologist or a superhero in order to make a difference. (Well, the birds may consider you a habitat hero.) Incorporating smart, bird-friendly plant choices is an easy way to make a difference, whether you have a lot of land, a postage-stamp size garden, or a balcony.

This book will explore ways you can make a difference for birds and enjoy the birds that visit your garden. You may even be motivated to inspire others to be an advocate for birds, as you will find with many of the profiled birder individuals in this book.

So let's get to the basics. To make your garden hospitable to birds, grow native plants which produce food in the form of seeds, fruit, nectar, and the insects they attract; and which offer safe places in which birds can hide and nest.

An American Goldfinch perches on a dried stem of non-native Oriental Poppy (*Papaver orientale*), surrounded by Rough Goldenrod (*Solidago rugosa*). As the goldenrod blooms, it will attract a large number of insects to feed on the pollen, which will then attract insectivorous birds. Once the flowering season is complete, the goldenrod blooms produce seeds that will attract finches, sparrows and juncos.

A Northern Mockingbird perches in a pine tree along the Northeast coastline.

All about Birds

Basic needs

Three main areas should be considered when making a garden or private property more bird-friendly:

- Will birds find suitable spaces to rear young or find cover?
- Will birds have access to food?
- Will birds have access to fresh water?

Cover encompasses the multitude of native evergreen and deciduous trees and shrubs that can provide birds a spot to nest or hide within. This can be accomplished through layered gardening (groundcovers, shrubs, and trees) or with a hedgerow. A hedgerow is a mixture of shrubs and trees that provide food as well as cover for birds. They are often planted along property borders. Some even serve as windbreaks.

A juvenile Tufted Titmouse hides inside the Spicebush (*Lindera benzoin*) branches.

Another informal cover option in a garden is a brush pile. This is a collection of branches and sticks piled on top of each other to provide pockets for birds to hunt for food (especially sparrows and wrens) as well as spots to hide if needed. Other wildlife may take advantage of brush piles, too.

ROLE OF NATIVE PLANTS AND INSECTS

Even though "feeding the birds" is synonymous with putting out bird feeders, the majority of a bird's diet is insects—especially when raising their young. You play a major role in creating safe areas for baby birds to be raised. In fact, 96 percent of land birds feed insects as the primary source of food to their young.

As the seasons change, being able to provide food from native plants (best suited for your area) is the best way to attract birds to your property. While exotic and native plants can look similar, they do not all serve the same purpose for wildlife. You may notice that many exotic species do not show any insect holes on their leaves at all. Plants native to North America will provide food for native insects—which means you may see more chewed leaves in the garden. But this is a great thing! Holes in leaves means native insects are present—which means food for songbirds.

Technically a native plant is one that has been present for hundreds or thousand of years in a particular region. Plants in the US are considered native if they occurred prior to European colonization. It has evolved with the wildlife and insects in the area, and sometimes it needs specific insects for pollination or birds to spread seeds.

Many of the native plants included in this book indicate the region it is native to—either Northeast, Southeast, Midwest, Southwest, or West. Plants native to your region will perform best.

Seeing how a plant grows in the wild and recreating those conditions in your garden can help set it up for success. However, despite good intentions, it may be that certain plants are not possible to grow due to the region you call home. For example, a southwest garden that contains many drought-tolerant plants that thrive in full sun and dry heat will not be happy in a humid region with more rainfall throughout the year. A purple coneflower (*Echinacea* spp.) that excels in a prairie setting will not be happy in a shade garden with ferns. Plus, the insects that call the shade garden home wouldn't know what to do with a coneflower—remember, native plants have evolved with wildlife and insects that are typically present there. Some native plants support specific insects and/or animals, such as the Golden-cheeked Warbler that nests exclusively in Texas using bark from the Ashe Juniper (*Juniperus ashei*) to build its nests.

Native plants are a food source for insects that are acclimatized to the region. Not all insects are fairly obvious for us to see—we may only notice the signs that they were present, such as holes in leaves. But these native insects play a vital role in providing food for birds.

While nature—and birds—are trying to adapt to our changing environment and climate, these adaptations do not take place quickly. Adding plants native to your region will help the birds in the area survive. As you begin to work native plants into your garden and landscape plans, you will find there is a lot of diversity—and generally there is a plant for every specific growing spot. In California alone, there are 6,500 native plant species—one-

Locate the native plants that will grow best in your backyard by entering your 5-digit zip code into the National Audubon Society Native Plants Database. Scan the QR code which will navigate you to the website.

A large portion of a bird's diet is insects. A female Red-winged Blackbird finds a caterpillar on a silver maple tree (*Acer saccharinum*).

A Northern Cardinal perches in a tall evergreen tree.

third of those plants are not found anywhere else on earth (California Native Plant Society).

Many independent garden centers have recognized the growing interest in choosing native plants for gardens and landscapes. Inquiring at your local garden center about stocking more plants native to your region helps to underscore this importance.

When adding native plants to your garden, be sure to consider adding native trees if possible. Native trees offer protection and food to birds—either because they attract insects or produce seeds or nuts the birds will eat. Entomologist Doug Tallamy refers to oak trees (*Quercus* spp.) as keystone plants because of the number of creatures that exist on that species alone. There are more than 90 species of oak in North America, which feed more than 500 caterpillar species. Worldwide, there are 557 species of oaks that feed over 900 caterpillars (Tallamy 2021). Without a keystone plant, the full potential of the habitat is not met. In fact, 75 percent of the insect food that birds need is produced by only certain plants. According to Tallamy, in most U.S. counties, oaks, cherries, willows, birches, hickories, pines, and maples are producing the largest number of insects needed to support animal populations (2021). When researching what type of native plant you can add to your property, if you are able to incorporate a keystone plant, you'll get even more value from it as it ages and hosts multiple forms of life.

ROLE OF PESTICIDES AND NEGATIVE EFFECTS ON HABITATS

Fewer native insects available on a property means less food for songbirds. Using pesticides to eliminate unwanted insects will also affect the beneficial insects that are on your property—not just the insects you find undesirable. An example is when gardens are sprayed to remove mosquitoes. The spray will not target just the mosquito, but will detrimentally affect many other insects as well, such as caterpillars which will become butterflies.

Pesticides do not discriminate; they will often kill all species of caterpillars, larvae, and insects. Birds will have even less food to choose from if chemicals are used in the garden.

Providing native plants to attract the insects that birds eat **will not work** if pesticides and herbicides are used in the garden.

Even the plants you purchase can affect the health and vitality of the garden. Plants grown with pesticides such as neonicotinoids will also cause problems in the food chain. Neonicotinoids (or neonics) are a type of pesticide that is systemic—when sprayed on plants, its chemicals leech into the soil. This results in those chemicals being absorbed by the plant and retained in its tissues, causing harm to insects and birds. This can also occur by coating the seeds with the chemical before it is even planted. The plant continues to draw up the chemicals as it grows.

Think of a cut stem of a white carnation sitting in a glass with blue food coloring. The plant will bring the blue dye up through its vascular tissues and disperse the dye throughout the plant—most notably in the flower in this example. Neonicotinoids work in a similar way.

Neonicotinoids have ties to harming bees, and also detrimentally affect birds when they eat the coated seeds. In one study by the University of Saskatchewan, researchers found that White-crowned Sparrows that consumed small doses of a neonic called *imidacloprid* suffered rapid weight loss and delayed migration—having a negative role in the birds' survival and ability to reproduce.

Invasive or non-native?

Non-native (or exotic) plants are also sometimes referenced by the term *invasive*, but not all non-native plants are invasive. Take for example, Big Leaf Hydrangea (*Hydrangea macrophylla*), which is native to Asia. Although it is not native to the U.S., it will not take over a garden like Purple Loosestrife (*Lythrum salicaria*) will. The Purple Loosestrife is considered invasive and non-native. What makes a non-native invasive plant so detrimental to local growing areas is the ability for the plant to multiply and expand without natural checks and balances in place to keep the population of the plant under control. Non-native invasive plants often steal growing areas from native plants, which may be slower to colonize an area than the invasive species (such as Japanese Knotweed, *Fallopia japonica*).

True native plants vs. cultivars

A cultivar is a plant that is bred by humans to favor one or more specific traits. This can include the size or growth habit, disease resistance, leaf color, bloom color/shape/size/timing, etc. The plant is then propagated so that those traits are maintained. Plant tags will often indicate if the plant is a straight, or true, species of a native plant, or a cultivar, which often denotes a name inside quotation marks. Some cultivars are included as options in the plant lists in this book, primarily because they may fit smaller growing spaces better than the true species.

There are thousands, if not tens of thousands, of cultivars of native species available in garden centers across the U.S. Some cultivars of natives aren't much different from the true native, but some are significantly altered, causing the plant to become less recognizable to insects, birds, and other wildlife, specifically if the bloom is altered.

Ecologists agree that some cultivars of natives may hold ecological value—at least more than exotics from the other side of the planet—but it is generally believed that the true native is best.

Garden Phlox (*Phlox paniculata*) is a native plant, but breeders have created many hybrids and cultivars of the straight species that focus on flower color and size.

What birds eat

Your garden can provide food to different types of birds. Here are some of the most common foods that various species eat.

Legend:

Caterpillars/larvae	Sugar water	Spiders
Bagged seed	Nectar	Tree sap
Plant seed	Smaller birds/eggs	Frogs/lizards
Berries	Suet	Fish
Tree seed/pine cones	Flying insects (gnats, etc)	Small mammals (rabbit, squirrel, etc)
Small fruit	Snakes	Carrion
Insects (beetles, ants etc)	Voles/mice	Waterfowl
Citrus	Nuts	Turtles

Chickadees & Titmice

Bushtits

Kinglets

Wrens

Thrushes

Vireos

Cardinals, Grosbeaks & Buntings

New World Sparrows

Blackbirds & Orioles

Nuthatches

Creepers

Waxwings

Finches

Woodpeckers

Crows, Magpies & Jays

Wood Warblers

Hummingbirds

Swallows

Swifts

Gnatcatchers

Tyrant Flycatchers

Pigeons & Doves

Mockingbirds & Thrashers

Falcons

Hawks & Eagles

Owls

Regional differences

The regional differences of available native plants also contribute to the variety of birds present in each region. While looking at a map of the continental United States, there are five main regions: the Northeast, Southeast, Southwest, Midwest, and West. To birds, these regions represent different habitats and ecosystems:

- Temperate Grasslands, such as the Great Plains. This is America's most endangered habitat, with more than 60 percent of native grasslands lost (360 million acres). According to the State of the Birds Report (2022), grassland birds have experienced the largest species decline since 1970. The main reason for population loss is due to habitat conversion, tree and shrub encroachment, and pesticide applications.

- Arid Land, which is primarily found in the Western U.S. It faces challenges such as fires, drought, invasive plants, development, unsustainable grazing, and energy extraction.

- Mature Forests, which provide nesting areas in undisturbed areas for specific species and Second-growth Forest, as found in the Northeast and the Northwest.
    - Western Forest: Five species have lost more than half of their population since 1970, including Tipping Point species such as Pinyon Jay and Rufous Hummingbird.
    - Eastern Forest: Forest restoration programs appear to be helping bird populations.

- Shrubland (or scrub), early succession habitats made up of shrubs and young trees.

Not specific to any one region, large areas of land dominated by single-crop agriculture and large lawns often replace shrubland or grasslands, which means less available space for birds to nest.

A Song Sparrow perches on a Riverbank Grape (*Vitis riparia*).

CONNECTING GREEN SPACES THROUGHOUT NORTH AMERICA

Small urban forests, such as greenway belts, city parks, cemeteries with mature landscapes, and forested stream banks play an important role in serving as "corridors" to connect birds to larger forest habitats and provide areas for migrating birds to refuel (Kress 2006). Doug Tallamy has popularized this idea further with the creation of the Homegrown National Park program, where U.S. residents are encouraged to modify their property to be welcoming to native insects and birds. By stitching these properties together on a map, more wildlife-friendly green space is available.

Greenways not only provide ways to conserve natural landscape and protect native species of plants and habitats for birds and animals, but they also provide people with open spaces that can serve as pathways for bicycling and walking—contributing to social well-being and stress relief (Flink as cited in Klocke 2020). Here are some stand-out greenways in the U.S.

- East Coast Greenway: connects 15 states from Maine to Florida with 3,000 miles of trails (700 of which are off-road).
- American Discovery Trail: runs horizontally across the continental U.S., split into a northern route (4,834 miles) and a southern route (5,057 miles).
- Georgia: 100-mile-long Chattahoochee River Greenway project.
- New York: 750-mile-long cross-state Empire State Trail.
- Oregon: 1,200 miles of bike trails and greenways in the Portland Metro region.

KEEPING TRACK OF THE BIRDS

Community Scientists—the term used to categorize the nature enthusiasts who track the species of insects and birds that they encounter—make a great contribution to data that scientists can use to spot population trends, migration and breeding patterns, and more.

The Christmas Bird Count is a yearly tally to record the number of bird species in an area. It began on Christmas Day in 1900, when ornithologist Frank M. Chapman proposed that people go out to count the birds for a "Christmas Bird Census" instead of the holiday tradition that hunters engaged in, called the Christmas "Side Hunt." The hunters would choose sides and go into the field with their guns. The largest pile on one of the sides would win.

Chapman and twenty-seven birders recorded ninety species on their first bird count, in various locations across the North American continent. The tradition continues each year between December 14 and January 5. Now tens of thousands of volunteers throughout the Americas brave snow, wind, or rain, and take part in the effort. Bird conservation organizations and researchers use the data collected to assess the health of early winter bird populations, and to help guide conservation action.

Another well-known bird census is the North American Breeding Bird Survey (BBS), which originated in 1966 with Chandler Robbins. Robbins came up with the idea of engaging birders, located in different regional habitats, on one day a year during the height of the breeding season. The volunteers would drive a half mile, stop and get out of the cars, then record all species heard or seen for three minutes. Data from this yearly count helped scientists discover that several species of birds that breed in eastern U.S. forests and winter in Latin America had declined steeply between the mid-1970s and mid-1980s. The group has also been able to track the decline in other bird groups, such as grassland species and aerial insectivores (Tangley 2014).

Other data is entered on a volunteer basis by community scientists, such as Project FeederWatch. Project FeederWatch is a program through The Cornell Lab of Ornithology that encourages individuals to log descriptions of their private property and then record the total number of bird species visiting their feeder that they see over a two-day span during the observation period from November through April.

The data from all of these reports help scientists and conservationists spot trends in bird populations, behaviors, and more. Who knew reporting data could be so much fun?

Providing fresh water throughout the year

Birds need access to fresh water and will seek out these sources. The easiest way to add fresh water to your garden area is by including a birdbath in your garden design. Adding a water feature also increases your chances of attracting birds that normally do not visit bird feeders to the garden space. Many of the insectivorous birds, such as warblers, will spend most of their time in shrubs and trees. One way to entice them to your garden is by offering fresh water.

There are several different types of birdbaths available, and the safest ones for birds offer a shallow basin to bathe and drink from (no more than 2 inches in depth). Birdbaths that are deeper than this are generally risky for birds to use, but can be modified to include flat stacking rocks to give birds a safer way to access the water. Birdbaths should also provide a rough area for birds to access while in the water. Smooth surfaces will be more slippery and birds will be less likely to use them if they cannot get a firm footing.

Adding a moving water element to the water feature, either with an electric water pump plugged into an outdoor outlet or with a solar-powered fountain, will help birds find the birdbath (thanks to the sound the moving water makes).

Offer an assortment of birdbath heights in the garden to attract a variety of birds. Choosing a birdbath mounted on a pedestal or at ground level depends on the surrounding area. Birdbaths on

A House Finch drinks from water droplets on the leaves of Pokeweed (*Phytolacca americana*).

pedestals will attract Gray Catbirds, Tufted Titmice, Summer Tanagers, Bohemian Waxwings, and finches such as House Finches, Lesser Goldfinches, and American Goldfinches. Avoid placing ground-level baths in areas that obscure the birds' view of the surrounding area while bathing—this can make birds (and other small wildlife) possible victims of cats. Ground-level birdbaths will attract birds such as White-throated Sparrows and Mourning Doves.

While fresh water is important throughout the seasons, providing unfrozen clean water for birds to drink from in the winter will not only help your resident birds, but may attract others in the area, such as White-crowned Sparrows and Eastern Bluebirds. Heated birdbaths can be plugged in with an outdoor-rated extension cord to an outdoor outlet (make sure to use a cord protector to keep the plugs dry). The options include a unit that can be inserted into an existing birdbath to keep water above freezing, or an entire basin that keeps the water temperature above freezing. Heated birdbaths can be at ground level, on a pedestal, or even mounted to a deck railing.

Birdbaths (in all seasons) are best located in an area where birds can spot any movement or threat from predators. Having shrubs or a tree line nearby (within 6 to 10 feet) for birds to escape to is beneficial if hawks are also residents in the area. Birdbaths can be located near bird feeders, but should not be set up directly underneath them because spent seed shells will definitely make their way into the water.

Providing clean sources of water for birds to drink and bathe in will help prevent disease. It's important to keep birdbaths clean and replace the water at least every other day—once a day if it is being actively used. Regularly changing the water also prevents mosquitoes from hatching eggs in the stagnant water. A bristle-brush can be used to scrub and clean the inside basin, as well as any rocks that are placed inside. Use a ratio of 1 part bleach to 10 parts water to clean dirty birdbaths, and rinse thoroughly. Another option to clean the birdbath is with a water and vinegar solution (9 parts water to 1 part vinegar). Rinse well.

Gray Catbirds will visit a pedestal birdbath to bathe.

Mourning Doves will visit a heated birdbath during the winter months. The heated birdbath keeps the water from freezing, which provides drinking water when other natural sources may be frozen.

Migration

Many of the birds present during the warmer seasons in North America are neotropical migratory birds. There are more than 300 species of these birds which breed in Canada and the United States during the summer months and spend the winter in Mexico, Central America, South America, or the Caribbean. While the majority of these birds are songbirds, there are also shorebirds, waterfowl, and raptors that also migrate.

Some songbird species travel short distances, such as the Gray Catbird, Black-capped Vireo, Lucy's Warbler, and the Painted Bunting. Other bird species who migrate further south include the Red-eyed Vireo, Purple Martin, Barn and Cliff Swallows, Cerulean and Connecticut Warblers, and the Scarlet Tanager.

Why do birds go to the trouble of traveling long distances? When it is winter in North America, the natural food sources of caterpillars, insects, fruit, and nectar are diminished or completely absent for birds. However, the food is plentiful in the tropics—being at its peak season—which is well worth the trouble of flying thousands of miles and competing with local species there.

Most birds migrate at night, using the stars to navigate. Flying under the cover of night also helps the birds avoid predators that could hunt them during the day. They will stop throughout their journey during the day to rest and fuel up, which is how rare bird visitors are sometimes spotted in gardens and natural areas during the fall and spring migration.

Birds rely on each other to migrate safely—even birds of different species. Migratory birds, such as Palm Warblers and Dark-eyed Juncos, will seek out residential birds, such as Chickadees & Titmice, to help them locate food at stopover sites. These mixed species flocks can contain up to ten resident birds with other migratory songbirds joining in. According to ornithologist David Allen Sibley, the songbirds understand the chickadees' warning calls and rely on the chickadees to watch for danger while they focus on foraging. Migrating birds often join up with local chickadees to find the best sources of food and water. (They may even lead them to your garden if you offer enough native plants to provide the food they eat!)

A flock of Cedar Waxwings seek food in native plantings.

Painted Buntings are one of many beautiful songbirds that migrate.

An American Goldfinch in an Elderberry (*Sambucus canadensis*) tree.

A female Scarlet Tanager pauses in a backyard garden during the fall migration. When spending the summer in North America for breeding, it will be found mainly in deciduous forests where oaks are common, but also in maple, beech, and other trees.

Bird superstar

The Ruby-throated Hummingbird weighs less than 0.2 ounces. For comparison, a U.S. quarter (25-cent piece) weighs 0.2 ounces! The Ruby-throated Hummingbird begins its fall migration in September along the eastern United States. It will fly **600 miles nonstop** across the Gulf of Mexico during its migration until it reaches the overwintering grounds in Mexico and Central America. Because of the long overwater flight, it's important for the birds to find food to eat and store energy for the long journey. Beginning in March, the hummingbird will begin to fly north, feeding from early season flowering plants along the way as it gradually makes its way back up the eastern coast of the U.S.

A Ruby-throated Hummingbird pauses in flight to feed from Jewelweed (*Impatiens capensis*) and Garden Phlox (*Phlox paniculata*) flowers.

Ruby-crowned Kinglet on a tree branch.

White-throated Sparrows are the most common bird to hit windows in Toronto, Canada; Chicago, Illinois; and Manhattan, New York, according to The American Bird Conservancy/2019 study (Winger, et. all).

Even though millions of birds successfully make the journey each year, it is still a dangerous adventure. In order to successfully survive the migration twice a year, the birds need to find suitable habitat in between—as well as avoid collisions with buildings and bright overnight lighting.

Birds can be thrown off course by light pollution caused by bright cities, street lights, and even cell towers, which makes it harder to see the stars. Birds are attracted to lights and can be trapped in cities filled with dangerous buildings and glass. Artificial lights can also impact the timing of migration as it disrupts the birds' biological clocks. For this reason, the risk of birds colliding with the reflective glass in buildings increases during the spring and fall migration periods, especially for species that call out to each other as they fly overnight, according to a 2019 study (Winger, et. all). The birds at highest risk for collisions with buildings and glass include Black-and-white Warblers, Hermit Thrushes, Brown Creepers, Dark-eyed Juncos, Common Yellowthroats, Ovenbirds, and White-throated Sparrows.

If the birds do manage to avoid collision overnight, bright overnight lighting can disorient birds and cause them to fly in circles until dawn. As the sun comes up, the birds may find themselves still in an area where surrounding glass buildings still pose a threat (along with other predators). (See page 40 for ways you can make glass windows in your home less deadly for all birds—not just the migrants.)

The Lights Out program, created by The National Audubon Society, is a national effort to reduce the number of bird deaths due to excess lighting at night. By convincing building owners and managers to turn off excess lighting, the skies are a bit safer for birds as they migrate to nesting and wintering grounds. One of the easiest things you can do is to turn off unnecessary lighting from 11 p.m. to 6 a.m. during peak bird migration periods (September 1 through November 15 and April 1 through May 31). BirdCast (birdcast.info) is an online resource that produces bird migration forecast maps. Colorado State University and The Cornell Lab of Ornithology produce the forecasts that display predicted nocturnal migrations of birds three hours after local sunset. The data is updated every six hours.

Migration explorer

The National Audubon Society's Bird Migration Explorer lets you interact with the migration pathways of songbirds, as well as raptors, shorebirds, waterbirds, and waterfowl. More than 450 species of birds are represented. Learn more about a species, the migratory birds at a specific location, or a conservation challenge birds face.

A Red-bellied Woodpecker visits a suet feeder in a small backyard garden.

Responsible purchases benefit birds

Many of the Neotropical songbirds that are sighted in North America during the summer will migrate and spend most of their lives "wintering" in Central or South America, and find their way to shade coffee farms.

Coffee is a crop that has been traditionally grown under the shade canopy of other trees. On shade-grown coffee plantations, the coffee is grown under the canopy of the forest, which provides cover and insects for food—ideal habitat for birds. In contrast, sun-grown coffee plantations are grown as a monoculture, with the forest canopy removed (deforestation). Sun-grown coffee plants are more vulnerable to disease and farmers use more pesticides.

A Golden-winged Warbler.

Laura Jackson is passionate about volunteering her time to educate her community about birds, climate change, and habitat protection. In 2015, Laura and a group of Juniata Valley Audubon Society members (Altoona, Pennsylvania) visited the farm of Honduran coffee farmer Emilio Garcia. He uses shade-grown coffee practices on his family-owned farm—which also provides much-needed habitat for Neotropical songbirds.

When purchasing coffee beans for home use, look for bags certified as shade-grown, which are stamped with seals such as "Rainforest Alliance Certified" or "Bird Friendly." Both of these certifications require

farmers to maintain or restore some level of canopy cover and prohibit the use of harmful pesticides, which limit prey for birds.

The Smithsonian Bird Friendly® certification is a slightly more rigorous standard that ensures there is a mix of foliage cover, tree height, and biodiversity available for migrating birds, and it also guarantees that the farmers will receive a premium for their product.

Certified shade-grown coffee still makes up a small part of the market, and can often be found through online retailers. If shade-grown coffee is not available near you, look for coffee labeled as organic, which at least bans the use of pesticides on the coffee beans.

Four main travel routes

When birds migrate, they follow a major flight path to move between their breeding grounds and non-breeding grounds. This flight path is often referred to as a flyway. In North America, there are four main flyways traveled by birds each spring and fall.

While the flyways are used by several species of birds, it does not represent a direct route, but a general pathway the birds use to reach their destination. Each main route follows the geography of the continent, as birds use natural land features such as mountain ranges, inland wetlands, or the country's coast lines to help guide their journey. Understanding which birds use which flyway helps birdwatchers estimate which birds will likely be migrating through their local area. Even weather patterns can play a role in the migration numbers throughout the season.

Here's what you need to know about each flyway:

PACIFIC FLYWAY

- Stretches from Patagonia, South America to the Aleutian Islands; contains the entire North American and South American Pacific coastline and extends to the Rocky Mountain range.
- Birds tend to overwinter in Mexico and Central America, and many seabirds, shorebirds, and waterbirds migrate into South America.
- Notable for migration stopover points in California, Utah, Oregon, and Washington for birds that are coming from Alaska, Yukon, and the Northwest Territories, and as birds head to summer nesting sites further points north.
- Examples of songbird species that use this flyway are the Western Tanager, Townsend's Warbler, Rufous Hummingbird, Hermit Thrush, and Purple Finch.

CENTRAL FLYWAY

- Stretches from Central America to Canada; contains the Great Plains and Texas, Kansas, Colorado, Wyoming, and Montana.
- Birds tend to overwinter in southern portions of North America and Central America. This flyway is important for long-distance migrants from the boreal and arctic regions that winter in the southern states.
- Notable for the Sandhill Crane migration, which gathers in large numbers in the Nebraska Sandhills each spring. Also the flyway used for 50 percent of North America's migratory waterfowl.
- Examples of songbird species that use this flyway are the Bobolink and Clay-colored Sparrow.

MISSISSIPPI FLYWAY

- The northern portion of this flyway stretches from the Gulf of Mexico, following the Mississippi, Missouri, and Ohio Rivers and extends to the Great Lakes region and Canada.
- When migrating south, the birds tend to overwinter in South and Central America.
- Notable for being an ideal travel route for ducks, geese, shorebirds, and waterbirds.
- Examples of songbird species that use this flyway include the Prothonotary Warbler and Yellow-billed Cuckoo.

ATLANTIC FLYWAY

- Stretches from Florida to Greenland; contains the entire North American Atlantic coastline.
- Birds tend to overwinter in the Caribbean or South America.
- Notable for large concentrations of shorebirds and waterfowl.
- Examples of songbird species that use this flyway include the Black-throated Blue Warbler, Cerulean Warbler, Wood Thrush, and American Redstart.

Safe feeder practices

As you incorporate more native plants into your garden space, setting up a bird feeder is a good way to lure birds to your property. But feeding birds with supplemental food in this way comes with responsibility. Feeders need to be kept clean to prevent the spread of disease. One of the most common diseases that can spread through feeders is House Finch eye disease (formally known as Mycoplasmal conjunctivitis), which can infect additional birds besides House Finches. There's also a chance for salmonellosis (caused by salmonella bacteria), aspergillosis (a fungal respiratory disease), and avian pox to spread through dirty feeders. It is always best to check with local authorities to see if it is safe to put out feeders when reports of avian flu is in the news.

Cleanliness matters when providing supplemental food for songbirds.

Overall, keeping feeders clean and food fresh can set you up for success. When choosing, look for one that is easy to disassemble for cleaning.

To clean seed and suet feeders, first remove any debris that is stuck on it. A bristled brush used for feeders comes in handy for this. The National Wildlife Health Center recommends cleaning feeders with a 10 percent bleach solution (1 part bleach mixed with 9 parts water), rinse well with plain water, and allow to air dry before refilling with food.

As for food, seed needs to be replaced if it has spoiled due to weather. The ground underneath feeders also needs to be kept clean—mainly by discarding leftover seed shells, spoiled seed, and wet or moldy seed to discourage unsanitary conditions that can make birds sick. Regular cleanliness under feeders can also help keep rodents away, which can unfortunately be drawn to excess food.

Hummingbird nectar feeders also come with specific cleaning requirements to keep birds healthy. In cooler weather, cleaning the feeder once a week is recommended. In hot weather, the feeder should be emptied and cleaned at least twice per week. In both cases, the food should be discarded and replaced. If the feeder is emptied very quickly in hot weather, clean the feeder every time it is empty. Avoid placing the feeder in hot, direct sunlight which can make the solution spoil faster.

Cleaning with hot tap water works well, or use a weak vinegar solution. Avoid using dish soaps, as this can leave harmful residue in the feeder. A small brush can help clean the feeding ports to ensure there is no residual mold that has built up inside. Moldy sugar water can be harmful and even fatal for hummingbirds.

When it comes to the food inside the hummingbird feeder, stay away from reddening chemicals and food dye. You can make your own "nectar" solution by using a 1:4 ratio of refined white sugar to tap water. (Such as ¼ cup of sugar in 1 cup of water.) **Do not substitute the white sugar with honey, corn syrup, powdered sugar (confectioner's sugar), or raw, unprocessed sugars to make the hummingbird food.** These other sugars can be harmful to hummingbirds because they can ferment more quickly.

Bring the solution to a boil and let it cool before filling the feeder. You can make a larger batch and refrigerate the extra solution. Bring the solution up to room temperature before refilling the feeder. Extra solution should be discarded if it appears the sugar water has "turned," which means that the sugar solution is looking cloudy.

Ant moats can be used to keep ants away from feeders. This is usually a cup that is filled with water and hung above the feeder to prevent access. Bee guards can help discourage yellow jackets and wasps from feeding on the hummingbird food as well.

Outdoor cats and the threat they pose to birds

Cats that have access to the outdoors are a big threat to birds. Cats were an introduced species to North America by humans, accompanying the earliest European settlers in the 1600s. These cats were brought on ships to protect food supplies from mice and other vermin.

Since cats stalk their prey, they are usually not seen until they are too close to birds and other small critters. They hide especially well in large plantings. Even well-fed cats will hunt and pounce on birds—including hummingbirds. "Un-owned" feral cats make up the majority of this data, but pet cats play a role, too. The U.S. Fish and Wildlife Service estimated that an average of 2.4 billion birds are killed by cats each year (2017).

A 2015 study in the United Kingdom also underscored how much pet owners downplay the number of birds cats kill (McDonald, et. all 2015), often putting the desire of the cat to be outside over the importance of protecting species. If pet cats are kept indoors, it reduces the likelihood of them being hit by cars, being poisoned, contracting diseases, getting into fights, or becoming a victim to another predator (coyotes, for example).

Indoors, cats can live seventeen years or more. The life expectancy of an outdoor roaming cat is between two to five years. Another study confirmed that even the presence of a cat near a nesting site was enough to alarm parent birds to behave in two ways. In order to prevent the cat from finding the nest, the parent birds visited the young less (reduction of food) or used alarm calls to signal the vicinity of the cat, which also alerted other predators to the location of the nest (Bonnington, et. all 2013).

The best solution? Keep cats indoors.

Cats pose a danger to birds in the garden.

PESTS AND PREDATORS

Feeders also come with a few additional risks that are not related to food hygiene. As mentioned earlier, rodents can be drawn to excess food underneath feeders.

Bird feeders can sometimes draw the attention of hawks, who will use the feeder area as possible hunting grounds for songbirds. If you find that bird feeders are attracting hawks, stop filling the feeders for a period of two weeks. The decrease in feeder activity should encourage the hawk to move along to other hunting grounds. Songbirds will still be able to find food during this downtime and will often return pretty quickly to feeders once they are refilled.

Raccoons may also be attracted to bird feeders. Specially created baffles mounted on feeder poles will help to discourage them from climbing up to investigate. (Baffles are usually round, clear, strong plastic domes when mounted above a bird feeder, or can be long, metal tubular shaped cones that are mounted below a feeder along the pole.) Black bears can also be a nuisance, and feeders should not be used during a significant portion of the year when bears are active in neighborhoods or rural yards. Some homeowners have luck in only offering food in bird feeders during the snowy season when black bears hibernate.

Of course, squirrels often come with the bird feeder territory. While there are also baffles to discourage them from raiding bird feeders, it is often easier to set up a separate area for squirrels to eat or only offer food that squirrels are not particularly fond of—such as safflower seeds. (But hungry squirrels will even eat this not-so-favorite food.)

Starlings and House Sparrows are introduced species in North America that can also overwhelm bird feeders. Specially constructed feeder guards will help deter starlings from robbing bird feeders, which are usually grid-like squares that are not large enough for the birds to fit through.

A Red-shouldered Hawk perches on power lines in a suburban neighborhood to hunt for small mammals and songbirds.

Nesting box basics

To be a good bird landlord, birds will need access to sturdy, clean nesting boxes that are mounted at the correct height. Nesting boxes mounted lower than 3 feet can make birds susceptible to predators. Attaching a predator guard to the pole that the birdhouse is mounted on will also help discourage raccoons and snakes from hunting birds and eggs.

The size of the nest box, along with its entrance hole, will accommodate different species. The most common diameters for songbirds are 1½ inches and 1¼ inches.

- 1½ inch diameters will attract: swallows, Carolina Wrens, Eastern and Western Bluebirds
- 1¼ inch diameters will attract: Downy Woodpeckers, titmice
- 1⅛ inch diameters will attract: chickadees

Additional considerations for a good nesting box include the height of the box above the ground or water, the depth of the box, the size of the floor, and the preferred surrounding habitat. For detailed plans and specifics on nesting boxes, check out *The Birdhouse Book* by Margaret A. Barker and Elissa Ruth Wolfson (2021). *The Birdhouse Book* explains how to build and place functional do-it-yourself bird homes that are safe and appropriate for more than twenty of the classic North American species, from wrens to raptors.

COMPETING SPECIES

House Sparrows and European Starlings are year-round residents in many North American locales, which gives them an advantage to available nesting boxes before migratory native birds, such as Eastern Bluebirds and Tree Swallows, return. Both House Sparrows and starlings are known to attack and kill other birds for nesting sites.

Purple Martins prefer to live in community settings, close to people and near open bodies of water.

Both species prefer to nest close to humans, so timing and proper placement of nest boxes are two ways to discourage them from nesting. Nest boxes can either be removed from their poles or have the entrance holes plugged until the preferred species arrives in the area. Removing House Sparrow nests from nest boxes is another way to discourage them, but they can be very persistent! Nest boxes will need to be checked and emptied daily until the House Sparrows move along.

Placement for birdhouses is important when attracting birds. Eastern Bluebirds, for example, prefer houses that face open countryside with a few trees and shrubs. Large lawns, pastures, golf courses, parks, and other open areas are ideal locations for placement. A nearby tree or fence (within 50 feet of the nest box) will provide a spot for fledglings to perch after their first flight (Kress 2006).

Purple Martins are another species of birds that will use nesting boxes to raise their young. They will use both dried gourds and specialized houses. These birds are the largest species of North American swallows, and eat a variety of insects, including beetles, moths, dragonflies, butterflies, horseflies, leafhoppers, and wasps.

The houses need to be mounted between 12 and 20 feet high and at least 40 feet away from overhanging limbs and buildings. The poles will need the option to be raised and lowered so they can be inspected and cleaned when needed. Purple Martins prefer to nest near an open body of water (within a half mile) and in large community settings, so multiple boxes or gourds will be especially attractive. This is another species where nest box timing is key to prevent House Sparrows and starlings from moving in—mount boxes when the first Purple Martin "scouts" arrive back to the area.

No matter what type of nesting box you add to your property, when nesting boxes are not in use, they should be cleaned and stored.

NEST PLATFORMS

Certain species of birds will not use nest boxes but will nest on a platform when available. This includes American Robins, Barn Swallows, and Mourning Doves. Robins will also scout out areas under building eaves, including porch lights (if they look sturdy enough!). Phoebes will also build nests under protected eaves, even if it is over a frequently used doorway.

Nesting shelves can be installed in areas outside the home or on other outbuildings—either in exposed or protected areas. Barn Swallows will also use platforms, but will also find spots in barns, under porches, and in abandoned buildings.

NESTS IN SHRUBS AND TREES

Birds that nest in trees and shrubs include robins, House Finches, and juncos. (They may even commandeer a decorative wreath on a door if it appears sturdy enough!) Northern Cardinals will frequently find evergreens to raise their young in. Vireos, warblers, and native sparrows will nest in shrubs and trees where the branches provide support—which can be challenging to find in areas heavily browsed by deer (Kress 2006).

An Eastern Phoebe pauses on a tree branch while hunting insects for food.

NESTS ON THE GROUND

There are many songbirds who prefer to nest near the ground, including Hermit and Wood Thrushes; Bobolinks; Horned Larks; and Eastern, Western and Chihuahuan Meadowlarks. Some species of sparrows and warblers will also seek out nesting areas near the ground, such as the Wilson's Warbler, the Orange-crowned Warbler, Field Sparrow, and the Ovenbird. Often these areas are also covered by some type of vegetation, or in berry and fern thickets.

Many of the birds that belong to grassland habitats also nest on the ground. This is not limited to the Midwest. It can also include hayfields, pastures, fallow fields, as well as agricultural lands, landfills, and even airports. This placement, especially in hayfields, pastures, and old fields, increases the threat from predators such as raccoons, skunks, snakes, and foxes.

NESTING MATERIALS

Materials for birds to build their nests with can be placed out in the garden. This includes chicken feathers, alpaca fur, and grapevine bark strips that can be placed inside an empty wire suet feeder or inside a willow ball for birds to select from. Undesirable nesting materials can also be used, such as when robins weave in pieces of plastic from discarded trash (another reason to pick up litter in your community).

A female (top) and male (lower)
American Goldfinch feed on anise hyssop
(*Agastache foeniculum*).

PART II

Bird-friendly Garden Projects

Many of the garden project ideas in this book can be adapted to your garden. After native plants are established in your new garden space, the area will require less maintenance over time as the plants fill in and flourish.

The new garden bed can have a "wild" naturalistic feel, or can be thoughtfully and strategically laid out to look more formal. Some thoughts to consider as you begin planning:

- Do you admire linear design, where two garden beds on either side of a path are equal size and reflect the same plantings on each side?

- Do you prefer curved beds with a variety of plantings that are not repeated throughout the garden?

- Do you wish to keep a small portion of grass for children and pets?

Sketching out how you want the new garden bed to look will help with the planning process. Other considerations include noting where the sun rises and sets and the path it takes over your property. This will help determine the type of sun exposure your plants will have. Determine what type of soil you have. A soil test will help with this. Many state agricultural extension centers will offer this service.

Take stock of what is on your property. Do you have existing mature trees that could provide cover and homes for woodpeckers and other birds? Do you have an endless lawn that is able to be broken down into smaller parcels by adding new garden beds? Or perhaps you have a fairly established garden, but it is filled with plants that are not native to your area, and as a result, it doesn't provide food for the current population of birds. Examples of exotic plants would be gardens filled with daylilies that bloom briefly or a spot under trees where (often invasive) Japanese pachysandra grows. Take the time to remove any and all invasive species from the garden space.

The easiest way to start attracting birds to your surrounding property—whether that consists of a small patio area in an urban setting or rolling acres of land—is to add native plants to existing areas and remove any invasive species. Before you notice the birds—you may notice something else—insects! But do not grab the pesticides. Remember, you want insects to come to your garden because they are a primary food source for the birds you are trying to attract. And it won't take terribly long for the birds to notice that there is something different. As the plants mature and age on your property, they will be even more attractive to birds because they will provide more opportunities to feed and house them.

Even if a non-native plant is bird-friendly, native plants are guaranteed to be a food source for insects that are acclimatized to the region. This *Viburnum* spp. looks like a North American variety, but is actually native to Asia.

Pileated Woodpeckers seek out mature trees to nest in.

Not every bird will visit your garden. Many birds only frequent certain habitats. (See page 20 for regional differences.) The garden projects in this book provide suggestions for an assortment of environments and habitats to attract birds to your property—providing them with food, shelter, and water. When choosing a garden project, take stock of your growing zone and ecosystem. An open grassland habitat will support different birds than a small urban balcony.

HOW TO ADAPT THESE GARDEN PLANS TO YOUR AREA

In the suggested plant tables included in the projects that follow, the native range of the continental United States is indicated as well as the USDA hardiness zone to help you decide if the plant, shrub, or tree is a possible candidate for your garden.

The native ranges are divided into the following five general categories:

- **Northeast**: Maine, New Hampshire, Vermont, Massachusetts, Connecticut, Rhode Island, New York, Pennsylvania, and New Jersey.
- **Southeast**: Maryland, Delaware, Virginia, West Virginia, North Carolina, Kentucky, Tennessee, South Carolina, Georgia, Alabama, Mississippi, Florida, Arkansas, and Louisiana.
- **Midwest**: North Dakota, Minnesota, Wisconsin, Michigan, Ohio, Indiana, Illinois, Iowa, Missouri, Kansas, Nebraska, and South Dakota.
- **West**: Montana, Wyoming, Colorado, Utah, Idaho, Washington, Oregon, Nevada, and California.
- **Southwest**: Arizona, New Mexico, Texas, and Oklahoma.

What about Alaska and Hawaii?

Alaska and Hawaii are not included in the suggested native regions for the included garden projects. For readers based in Alaska, the USDA Hardiness Zones can be taken into consideration when choosing similar plants. For Hawaii, many of the birds are listed under the U.S. Endangered Species Act, and find refuge in high-elevation forests. Hawaiian forest bird recovery programs such as mauiforestbirds.org and kauaiforestbirds.org are working to protect endangered native birds such as the emblematic I'iwi (Scarlet Honeycreeper), the Kiwikiu (Maui Parrotbill), and the Puaiohi (Small Kaua'i Thrush). Local Hawaiian organizations are also working to conserve native Hawaiian plants. You can do your part by supporting local conservation efforts and planting native species in your garden to attract pollinators. Learn more about ways to contribute, and find listings of appropriate native Hawaiian plants, at nativehawaiianplantsociety.org, nativeplants.hawaii.edu, laukahi.org, and pepphi.org.

The 'I'iwi (Scarlet Honeycreeper) is protected as a threatened species under the Endangered Species Act. It is also an important pollinator, as it regularly drinks nectar from a wide variety of native plants.

SOURCING PLANTS

When purchasing plants for your garden, look for native plants that are labeled neonicotinoid-free. Inquire with plant nurseries to find out how their sources grow their stock plants. Plants started from seed in your region will also do better acclimating to your garden space. Look for labels such as *locally grown* which shows that that the plants were not trucked in from long distances (and possibly different regions). A native plant grown in your region will adapt better in your garden than one from a different part of the country.

Check out the plant tag for care information, too. Look for the growth dimensions of the plant and the conditions it tolerates. Does it like wet feet? Dry soil? When checking to see which plants are native to your area, look for those characteristics. For example, even if Serviceberry (*Amelanchier canadensis*) does not grow in your area, look for the size and growing conditions Serviceberry favors when substituting another local native plant or shrub for your growing zone.

Let's get started!

To see which birds will be attracted to the plants included in the following plans, check out the "Birds attracted" section. These icons indicate which birds find these plants desirable and may visit, depending on your geography. Use the key below to help navigate.

Chickadees & Titmice

Bushtits

Kinglets

Wrens

Thrushes

Vireos

Cardinals, Grosbeaks & Buntings

New World Sparrows

Blackbirds & Orioles

Nuthatches

Creepers

Waxwings

Finches

Woodpeckers

Crows, Magpies & Jays

Wood Warblers

Hummingbirds

Swallows

Swifts

Gnatcatchers

Tyrant Flycatchers

Pigeons & Doves

Mockingbirds & Thrashers

Owls

Hawks & Eagles

Falcons

A female Northern Cardinal eats berries from American black elderberry (*Sambucus canadensis*).

How to prevent window strikes: Modifying glass windows to be safer for birds

Large, clean windowpanes can make a home look welcoming and inviting. While people can see the glass and realize that the scenery that shows in certain lighting is just a reflection, birds cannot. Window collisions are one of the leading direct human causes of bird mortality.

The threat exists either during the day or night. During the day, glass can reflect the surrounding landscape in windows—including trees and vegetation—which birds can mistake as a safe spot to fly toward. Research indicates that up to one billion birds may be killed per year in the United States alone as a result of collisions, many which actually occur in low-rise buildings, rather than skyscrapers. The risk of birds colliding with reflective glass increases in the spring and fall due to the migration (see page 26 to learn more), with the main hazards contributing to these collisions being artificial light at night and glass. Impact with the glass can severely injure birds or be a cause of death—due to the force of impact or if a stunned bird is unable to escape a nearby predator.

Of all the windows in the home, large picture windows and windows that are adjacent to each other at right angles are the most dangerous windows for birds. If possible, these should be modified first.

While reflectivity is a major problem for birds, transparency of glass is also a cause of collisions. One way to mitigate the transparency of the glass window at night is to draw shades, blinds, and curtains. However, this is not as effective during the day because these window dressings intensify the reflective quality of the glass.

Window decals can be applied to glass windows, which will help birds "see" the "break" in the window reflection. This photo illustrates how the vertical dotted tape—spaced in rows 1½ inches apart—helps break up the reflection in the top left windowpane. The top right windowpane is not treated with decals or tape and shows the full reflection of the trees in the distance. Both windowpanes have an outdoor screen mounted on the bottom portion of the window, which helps to also break up the reflection.

Unfortunately, sounds or smells cannot be used to help prevent collisions. However, there are glass products commercially available to help prevent collisions. These include using acid-etched glass (which provides a frosted appearance) and fritted glass (glass printed with ink, especially on the outermost surface).

TIME TO GET CREATIVE

Luckily, there are ways to make glass windows safer for birds as they move through your property. The following modifications can be added to windows:

- Tempera paint applied to the outside surface of the glass can be used to create a grid pattern. Or the paint can be used to draw patterns and designs. The paint is non-toxic and easy to use.

- Hang netting or cords in front of the glass window. Netting should not contain open spaces that are larger than 2 × 2 inches. Hanging cords should be spaced no wider than 4 inches apart. When placed at these intervals, both netting and cords can discourage most birds from trying to fly through them into the glass.

- Vinyl dots can be applied as a pattern on windows, making it easier for birds to see.

- Window tape or window film can be applied to the outside portion of a glass window pane, and is available in a variety of sizes.

- Screens that are mounted on the outside portion of a window will also help reduce reflections.

When applying paint, leave no more than 2 inch spacings between each design or decal. The repetitive pattern will be beneficial for creating a warning sign for birds.

Singular decals placed in only one spot of the window will not warn birds of the larger, reflective portion of the glass. Attaching a hawk or raptor silhouette to a window or other nature designs are not effective in discouraging birds from hitting the glass because of the number of decals and silhouettes needed to warn birds.

Ola Rucz is an artist based in Connecticut who designs and paints glass windows for town buildings and shops. Many of her designs are hand-drawn on windows with paint markers. These designs have the additional benefit of breaking up reflections in the glass that may confuse birds. More of her work can be found at Instagram.com/art_by_ola.

Tips for safely photographing birds

Birds are popular subjects for photos, and modifying your garden and property to be more inviting to birds will increase your chances of taking photos at home. There are two main things to keep in mind when taking great bird photos: follow ethical guidelines as you photograph birds and be familiar with your surroundings.

PUT THE BIRDS FIRST

It's important to not stress birds in an attempt to get the perfect photo or video. **The well-being of the birds and their habitats must come first.** When photographing birds, keep the following in mind:

- Be patient and study the birds' behavior before photographing them. Knowing them will allow you to anticipate their moves.
- Be aware of the surroundings and if predators, such as hawks or cats, are present.
- Place feeders near an area where you can see them clearly, such as by a nearby porch or garden bench.

Being present and observant will help you capture moments such as this, where an Eastern Bluebird feeds on seeds.

WHAT NOT TO DO:

- **Do not get too close** to nests by using a short lens to photograph. Use a long lens and crop in a digital program in post-editing instead. Also, do not remove anything, including branches or limbs, that obscures the nest from predators in order to get a clearer photo.
- **Do not capture birds** and force them to pose in a controlled environment. Birds should be kept wild.
- **Do not bait owls, hawks, or other raptors with mice** or other food sources to lure them to an area for a photograph. This can promote disease and habituate the birds to humans.
- **Do not use a camera flash**, especially at night, which can temporarily distract or blind nocturnal birds.
- **Do not use playback of bird calls** to draw birds out. When a bird leaves the nest to pursue or defend their territory from a perceived challenger or predator, eggs and/or chicks are left open to predation and weather conditions.
- **Do not share the location** when sharing your photos on social media if your garden or property is home to a rare bird, especially if it is of a nesting bird or a raptor (such as an owl).

ACCESS TO PHOTOGRAPHY EQUIPMENT

- **Borrow.** If you do not own a camera, ask a family member or friend if they have a camera they would be willing to loan you.
- **Old is new again.** Check out refurbished cameras or lenses, which means the camera was returned for repair but will work the same—at a lesser cost.
- **Renting.** If you want to splurge on a long lens to capture harder-to-spot birds, such as migrating warblers, look into renting a camera lens online.
- **Use your smartphone with a camera shutter remote.** Another option is setting up your smartphone on an appropriate stand or mount

to record video. If birds visit an outside patio or balcony area, or a hummingbird feeder, you can set your smartphone up with a camera shutter remote to take photos when the birds come close to the smartphone. This does not require you to be holding the smartphone to take the photo.

- **You can also combine your smartphone with a spotting scope or binoculars.** Referred to as "digiscoping" you can combine an adapter to the eyepiece of the spotting scope or a binocular adaptor to the eyepiece of binoculars. Both will hold the smartphone in place to take an image. Using a tripod makes the process easier as well.
- **Look into blinds or hides.** These camouflaged tents provide a place for the photographer to "hide" from birds, allowing you to get a little closer to your garden birds. Keep the blind out for some time before using it, so the birds will get used to seeing it in the garden.

COMPOSITION TIPS

In the warm season, the best times to photograph birds are in the early morning and early evening. Birds are most active at these times as they search for insects to eat. During the middle of the day, songbirds may be trickier to find since they may be hiding from predators or resting in the cover of a shrub or tree.

In the colder season, you are more likely to see birds throughout the day if you provide seed or suet with a bird feeder (be sure to keep it clean).

However, your garden may attract large numbers of birds if you offer native shrubs and trees that produce fruit that remains for the majority of the season. Dogwood trees (*Cornus florida*), and viburnums (*Viburnum* spp.) are two examples that may attract American Robins or Cedar Waxwings.

When it comes to composing the photo, keep the following in mind:

- Incorporating medium to larger size shrubs and trees within your camera's viewfinder will provide natural areas for birds to perch, besides fences and railings.
- Position yourself so the bird is not directly in front of the sun. If the sun is behind the bird, it will create a silhouette image, but will obscure the details (such as feathers).
- In post-production, do not crop in too closely on the finished image. Leaving some of the available environment in the photo helps provide context for the habitat the bird is in and provides visual interest.
- Avoid using high ISO settings when photographing birds in darker environments. ISO refers to the sensitivity to light, either on film or of a camera's sensor. (Ideally using an ISO of 100 will help increase the image's quality.) The ISO setting on a camera will brighten or darken a photograph. Higher ISOs settings will brighten an image, but they can also introduce a grainy look—or "noise"—to the image.

Cropping in on a photo (right) provides a bit more detail on the bird, but still includes some environment in the shot to help provide context for the habitat the bird was found in.

Drought-tolerant garden featuring native grasses

Native grasses play an important role in the various ecosystems in North America. Not only do they provide the three things birds need from plants—food, cover, and nesting materials—they also provide ecological benefits, such as minimizing erosion due to water and wind. Not surprisingly, natural grassland offers more to insects than turfgrass and lawns. (In fact, the roots of many native grasses extend deeper into the soil than turfgrass.)

This wildlife benefit is not the only perk that makes native grasses desirable in landscapes and gardens. They add color, movement, and interest to garden design and plantings.

Prairies are one of the main habitats for native grasses, which used to cover nearly one third of North America, according to the National Park Service. The prairie stretched as far north as Saskatchewan, Canada and south to Texas. The different varieties of grass that ranged between the Rocky Mountains and east of the Mississippi River were made up of varying heights, depending on the average rainfall in the area. This consisted of three main regions:

- **Tallgrass prairie** produced grass as high as 8 feet tall, due to 30 inches or more of annual rainfall.
- **Midgrass prairie** produced a mixture of grass heights, with a range of 12 to 30 inches of annual rainfall.
- **Short-grass prairie** incorporated shorter grasses that provide little cover, due to 10 to 15 inches of annual rainfall.

Warm-season grasses are mixed with other drought-tolerant native plants in this large, converted stock tank, complete with drainage holes.

COOL VS. WARM

Native grasses can be incorporated into existing garden beds or planted exclusively into a new garden bed or container garden. When planted in a large area and in large groupings, native grasses can provide cover for birds to hide from predators. The seedheads provide food to a variety of birds into the colder seasons, and the long grass blades provide nesting materials. Most can tolerate poor soil but the plants do have a variety of water requirements, depending on their species. Native grasses can be found throughout the United States, and are generally divided into two categories: cool season and warm season.

Cool-season grasses are the first to grow in early spring. They tend to stay greener into the fall and may go dormant during the height of summer's high temperatures.

Warm-season grasses are the varieties that stay green during the hotter temperature months, and will turn brown as the cool season sets in. They are typically more drought-tolerant. The grasses used in the container on the previous page planting focus on warm-season grass varieties.

The purple flowers of Meadow Blazing Star (*Liatris ligulistylis*) are very attractive to monarch butterflies. Let the flowers go to seed and remain standing—birds will feed on the seeds.

GRASSES ADAPT WELL TO LARGE CONTAINERS

For those with limited space, or mainly access to paved areas, this full-sun garden plan is big on color and structure. Stock tanks, such as the one used for this project, can be found at agriculture supply stores, and serve as a large impact statement planter. (Just remember to install the proper drainage holes with a drill). The stock tank used to grow these native plants was an oval 40-gallon tank (2 feet by 4 feet by 1 foot). To make this or any other large container garden portable, set it up on casters before filling it with soil and plants. (Moving furniture dollies also work very well!)

While grasses are the stars of this garden plan, other plant species are interplanted with them, providing visual interest beginning in early summer and lasting into the winter. When pairing plants, choose ones that share similarWater needs and are bird-friendly. Be sure to provide consistent moisture through the first year of growth to set the plants up for success.

Native Common Yarrow (*Achillea millefolium* var. *occidentalis*) is a great addition to a water-wise garden plan, and once established, it is fairly drought-tolerant. Some cavity-nesting birds will use yarrow to line their nests, and will eat the seeds and many of the insects attracted to the plant. Leaving the grasses standing throughout the winter months will provide seeds for birds to eat, and can be cut back in late winter/early spring to make room for new growth. The seeds of White Heath Aster (*Symphyotrichum ericoides*) will attract birds such as American Goldfinches, Black-capped Chickadees, Dark-eyed Juncos, Eastern Towhees, Northern Cardinals, and White-breasted Nuthatches.

Remember: While many non-native grasses originating from Asia are sold in U.S. nurseries (especially in the fall), ask your garden center to stock native varieties local to your region for use in your garden spaces.

Plant name	Plant size	Water needs	Preferred lighting conditions	Hardy to (USDA zones)	Provides			Main season of interest	Native range
Common Yarrow (*Achillea millefolium* var. *occidentalis*)	1 to 3 feet tall and wide	Dry soil	Full sun to part shade	3b-11	✓		✓	Summer flowers attract an assortment of insects that birds will eat, in addition to the seeds.	Throughout North America
Meadow Blazing Star (*Liatris ligulistylis*)	3 to 5 feet tall	Average to dry soil	Full sun	3-6	✓			Flowers attract hummingbirds. Seeds feed birds in late summer, early fall.	Midwest
White Heath Aster (*Symphyotrichum ericoides*)	Up to 3 feet tall	Moist to dry to well-drained soil	Sun	5-8	✓			Very attractive to native insects. Seeds feed birds in winter.	Midwest, Northeast
Smooth Aster (*Symphyotrichum laeve*)	1 to 3 feet tall	Moist to dry well-drained soil	Sun	5-8	✓			Late summer to early fall blooms. Attracts many native insects.	Midwest, Northeast, Southeast, Southwest
Yellow Coneflower (*Echinacea paradoxa*)	24 to 30 inches tall	Well-drained, lean soil	Full sun	5-8	✓			Attracts hummingbirds and seed-eating birds.	Midwest
Wand Panic Grass (*Panicum virgatum*)	3 to 6 feet tall	Dry to moist soil	Full sun to partial shade	5-9	✓	✓	✓	Attractive to butterflies. Provides cover, food and nesting material for ground-feeding and game birds.	Northeast, Southeast, Midwest, Southwest, partial West

ALSO CONSIDER FOR YOUR REGION

Plant name	Plant size	Water needs	Preferred lighting conditions	Hardy to (USDA zones)	Provides			Main season of interest	Native range
					✿	♠♠	≝		
Deergrass (*Muhlenbergia rigens*)	3 to 4 feet tall	Low	Full sun	7-10	✓		✓	Birds eat seeds. Foliage is used for nests.	Southwest
Little Bluestem (*Schizachyrium scoparium*)	18 to 24 inches tall and 12 inches wide	Low	Sun to part shade	3-9	✓	✓	✓	Color changes from blue green to red in fall into winter. Will spread in larger landscapes. Seeds feed birds.	Northeast, Midwest, West, Southwest, Southeast
Blue-stemmed Goldenrod (*Solidago caesia*)	1 to 3 feet tall and 1 to 1.5 feet wide	Average to dry	Full sun to part shade	4-8	✓			Larval host plant for insects. American Goldfinch eat the seeds.	Midwest, Northeast, Southeast

The prairie ecosystem

Did you know? The prairie ecosystem is one of the most complicated and diverse ecosystems in the world, surpassed only by the rainforests in Brazil. Now this ecosystem is one of the rarest and most endangered (Source: The National Park Service).

Common Yarrow (*Achillea millefolium* var. *occidentalis*) is native to most of the continental United States. The white flowers are flat-topped, which makes it easier for insects to land on and feed. It blooms throughout the growing season.

BIRDS ATTRACTED

Cardinals, Grosbeaks & Buntings

Woodpeckers

Mockingbirds & Thrashers

Crows, Magpies & Jays

Chickadees & Titmice

Finches

Waxwings

Vireos

Blackbirds & Orioles

Wood Warblers

New World Sparrows

Grow your own birdseed

Afun way to offer birdseed for the upcoming colder season is to grow your own. Two flower seeds that are popular with songbirds include sunflowers and coneflowers. Sunflower seed is sold in a variety of stores, is used in many bird feeders, and is popular with Northern Cardinals, Tufted Titmice, American Goldfinches, and other songbirds. Tall purple/pink coneflowers are also popular with birds, but are not harvested in the same way as sunflower seeds. Coneflower stems can be left standing as the flowers fade and seeds ripen. As the season turns cooler, birds, especially finches, will be drawn to the seeds.

HOW TO START SUNFLOWERS

Sunflowers (*Helianthus annuus*) are one of the iconic flowers that are associated with summer, sunshine, happiness—and are a popular source of bird food! Sunflowers have been bred to come in various flower sizes and petal colors. They can grow from 2 to 8 feet tall, and include one large flowerhead, or several branches with flowers ranging in size. For sunflowers being grown as birdseed, skip the seed varieties that are labeled "pollenless"—these will not produce seed.

Sunflower seeds are large and easy to handle, so planting the seeds can be a fun activity for children to participate in. Once the danger of frost has passed in your growing region, seeds can be directly sown into the warm soil (either in a raised bed, directly into the ground, or in a large container). Follow the seed packet instructions when planting. To protect the seeds from hungry chipmunks, cover the area with tuille or a lightweight garden cloth, and secure the fabric loosely with plant staples to the soil. (Leave a little room at the top of the fabric for the plant to grow upward.) Plant staples can be purchased in a package and are used to secure fabric to the ground. The sunflower seeds can also be planted under a do-it-yourself hoop house, which uses curved wire to support the lightweight cloth and

Purple Coneflower (*Echinacea purpurea*) is a popular native perennial that attracts butterflies to the garden. Songbirds will feed on the seedheads that are left standing in the garden during the fall and winter.

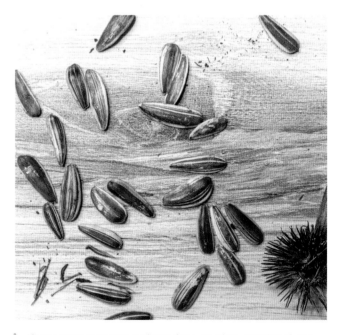

If you want numerous plants for a garden, starting them from seed is often cheaper than purchasing mature ones.

provide protection for the plant. This can be used longer than just placing the cloth on top of the small seedlings since it allows more room for the plant to grow vertically.

The seedlings will grow quickly with direct sunlight. Check the seed packet for how long it will take the sunflower to bloom. On average, they bloom between eleven and eighteen weeks from sowing the seeds. Birds, mainly goldfinches, will find the sunflowers and begin feasting as soon as the seeds begin to ripen. This is a wonderful opportunity to observe the birds as they harvest ripened seed from each flower.

If you prefer to save the seed for use over the winter months, cover the aging sunflower head with a brown paper bag or cheesecloth and secure it with a piece of jute or string. This will allow the seeds to ripen without being disturbed, and allows the plant to "breathe" through the bag. (A plastic bag would heat up and possibly cause the seedheads to become too moist and risk rotting in the sun.)

HOW TO START CONEFLOWERS

Narrow-leaf Coneflower (*Echinacea angustifolia*) and Purple Coneflower (*Echinacea purpurea*) seeds can be sown in the fall. *E. angustifolia* needs exposure to colder temperatures for at least ninety days in order to sprout the following spring (this is called **cold moist stratification**). *E. purpurea* will germinate after being sown in a warm location, but can also be sown in the fall. Because coneflowers are a perennial, plants grown from seed may not produce flowers in the first year. However, coneflower seeds can also be started in late summer and overwintered in a greenhouse or protected area outside—this may give them a jump start in blooming.

There are a few options for starting coneflowers from seed:

- If you have a prepared garden bed, scatter the seeds on the soil in the fall and cover lightly with a sand/soil mixture.
- You can also sow the seeds in a mixture of moist sand/soil in small seed starting containers and place them inside a protected greenhouse outdoors.

A male American Goldfinch searches for sunflower seeds from a blooming plant.

Sunflowers (*Helianthus annuus*) going to seed.

- Seeds can be sown inside a plastic container (such as a gallon milk jug) in late fall and left outside in a protected area to cold stratify. Cold stratification is the process of exposing seeds to cold and moist conditions to encourage germination after a certain period of days. (Seeds can also be sown in moist sand/soil).

- If leaving the seeds outdoors in the colder months is not an option, you can sow the seeds in the soil mixture inside a plastic bag and place the bag inside the fridge for about ninety days.

HOW TO SOW SEEDS IN PLASTIC CONTAINERS ("WINTER SOWING")

You will need work gloves, a box cutter, seed starting soil, duct tape or plastic wrap, and coneflower seeds.

Step 1: Clean the selected container with dish soap and rinse thoroughly. Remove the plastic cap.

Step 2: Wearing work gloves, turn the container upside down and using a box cutter, slice four 1-inch slits in the bottom in an "x" pattern.

Step 3: Turn the container right-side up and measure an inch and half from the bottom. Mark with a pen or marker around the circumference of the container.

Step 4: Using the box cutter, slice along the marked line, leaving a 2-inch gap in the back. This gap will form a hinge to bend the plastic cover backwards.

Step 5: Fill the container with the moist soil/sand mixture, leaving a half-inch gap at the top of the cut plastic. Sow the coneflower seeds on top and lightly cover with the soil mixture.

Step 6: Fold the plastic top hinge back down so it is sealing off the plastic jug. Using plastic cling wrap or duct tape, seal the container along the cut edges so it is closed.

Step 7: Place your container in a protected spot outside that will receive some sunlight and moisture, but is not in direct sun or under a drain spout or deck edge where runoff water can flood the container during heavy storms. You can let snow naturally cover the container as well.

Sowing seeds inside a clear plastic jug or container can be used to protect the seedlings from the elements and expose them to the required cold stratification days needed to sprout.

Step 2: Milk jug turned upside down to show how to cut with box cutter.

Step 8: Check your containers periodically as the temperatures warm in the spring. Seedlings can remain in the plastic container until the plant is about 2 inches tall. At this time, they can be removed from the container and planted in a large seed container or in a protected part of the garden to continue to grow.

Step 4: Bend back the plastic top so it is still attached and fill with soil/sand mixture.

Step 5: A sealed winter sowing container in a protected spot.

BIRDS ATTRACTED

Crows, Magpies & Jays

Chickadees & Titmice

Waxwings

Woodpeckers

Mockingbirds & Thrashers

Cardinals, Grosbeaks & Buntings

Nuthatches

Wrens

Finches

Thrushes

New World Sparrows

🌼 = Food 🌲 = Cover 🪺 = Nesting Material/Site

THIS GROW YOUR OWN BIRDSEED PLAN FEATURES THE FOLLOWING NATIVE PLANTS

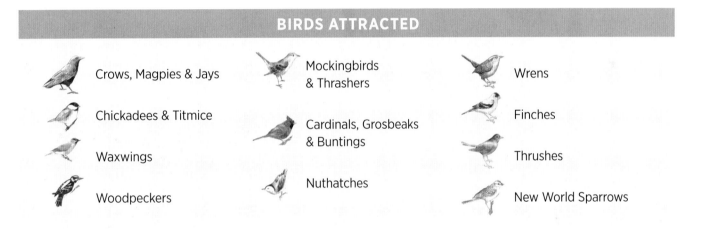

Plant name	Plant size	Water needs	Preferred lighting conditions	Hardy to (USDA zones)	🌼	🌲	🪺	Main season of interest	Native range
Common Sunflower (*Helianthus annuus*)	5 to 10 feet tall	Dry clay soil or heavy sand	Full sun	2-11	✓			Flowers can be enjoyed throughout the summer and birds will begin to harvest seeds as soon as they ripen.	All U.S.
Purple Coneflower (*Echinacea purpurea*)	2 to 4 feet tall and 2 feet wide	Dry, well-drained soil	Full sun to part shade	4-9	✓			Blooms early summer through fall, produces seeds for birds. Also attractive to butterflies and native bees.	Midwest, some Southeast, Northeast
Narrow-leaf Coneflower (*Echinacea angustifolia*)	1.5 to 2 feet tall	Well-drained soil, drought-tolerant	Sun to part shade	3-8	✓			Blooms April through June.	Midwest, some Southwest, and some West

Fruit garden for the birds

Many of the fruits that we enjoy eating are also attractive to songbirds. This garden focuses on different layers of vegetation available throughout the year. While the majority of the plants produce fruit during the warmer season, Highbush Cranberry (*Viburnum opulus* var. *americanum*) will hold on to the fruit into the winter, and won't be palatable to birds until it has been frozen and thawed a few times.

Begin with at least three plants of the low-growing groundcovers. Start with low-growing Red Bearberry (*Arctostaphylos uva-ursi*), Virginia Strawberry (*Fragaria virginiana*) or Pilgrim Cranberry (*Vaccinium macrocarpon* 'Pilgrim'), both which can form an attractive groundcover once established. Red Bearberry is more appropriate if the garden spot is drier (and can be incorporated around existing large rocks if present). Pilgrim Cranberry is happiest in moist, sandy areas. Virginia Strawberry can tolerate both conditions, and will spread by runners (as opposed to the other two groundcovers, which will slowly expand in size). All will spread over time, which will help create a layer of vegetation that will protect the soil, help combat and prevent erosion, and slow evaporation during hot spells. Mix and match the plants to create multiple foliage textures, or choose one variety if a uniform layer is more desirable.

For the shrubs, include a minimum of two of each variety, which works well in medium to large gardens. (Larger gardens can increase the number to three or five or each, depending on the available space.) The Black Elderberries, Highbush Blueberries and Highbush Cranberry will need at least two plants present in order to produce more fruit.

Consider incorporating both Highbush Blueberry (*Vaccinium corymbosum*) and Lowbush Blueberry (*Vaccinium angustifolium*) into your garden, which will produce food at different times during the growing season.

A Gray Catbird scouts for ripe blueberries in a Highbush Blueberry (*Vaccinium corymbosum*) shrub.

The berries of Highbush Cranberry (*Viburnum opulus* var. *americanum*) will turn red in late fall but are usually not eaten by birds until later in the season.

A Highbush Blueberry (*Vaccinium corymbosum*) with berries beginning to ripen. In the fall, the green leaves will turn a brilliant shade of red.

If adding a large American Black Elderberry (*Sambucus canadensis*) is not possible in your space, consider adding the shorter growing Black Chokeberry (*Aronia melanocarpa*) instead. This shrub will not get as tall as the elderberry and will hold on to the fruit longer throughout the season.

Elderberries and blackberries will attract Rose-breasted and Black-headed Grosbeaks.

Once the birds discover the food source, they will visit multiple times a day. If you also want some share of the ripening fruit (blueberries or strawberries), it's recommended to plant extra plants. Bird netting for specific blueberry shrubs works successfully when it is correctly mounted to a frame or cage that surrounds the plants. Draping the netting over the shrub itself can lead to birds getting their feet tangled, and is not recommended. For strawberries, placing a floating fabric row cover and securing with earth staples after the flowers have been pollinated is one way to ensure you get first pickings.

BIRDS ATTRACTED

- Mockingbirds & Thrashers
- Chickadees & Titmice
- Thrushes
- Woodpeckers
- Blackbirds & Orioles
- Finches
- Crows, Magpies & Jays
- Cardinals, Grosbeaks & Buntings
- Waxwings
- New World Sparrows
- Kinglets
- Wrens
- Nuthatches
- Creepers
- Vireos

Black Chokeberry (*Aronia melanocarpa*) provides visual interest in the garden and food for the birds. They have a bitter flavor and are high in Vitamin C—a good source of energy for birds when food can become scarce.

American Black Elderberry (*Sambucus canadensis*) is attractive to a variety of birds, including robins and House Finches.

THIS FRUIT GARDEN FOR THE BIRDS PLAN FEATURES THE FOLLOWING NATIVE PLANTS

Plant name	Plant size	Water needs	Preferred lighting conditions	Hardy to (USDA zones)	Provides			Main season of interest	Native range
					✿	▲▲	♨		
Highbush Blueberry (*Vaccinium corymbosum*)	6 to 12 feet high and wide	Dry to wet soil	Full sun to shade	4-8	✔			Fruit in late July/August. Red leaves in autumn.	Northeast, Southeast, some Southwest
Red Bearberry (*Arctostaphylos uva-ursi*)	6 to 12 inches tall and 6 feet wide	Dry to moist spots	Full sun to shade	2-6	✔			White and pink flowers in spring attract hummingbirds. Berries attract songbirds and ground-feeding birds.	Northeast, Southeast, some Midwest, some West
Virginia Strawberry (*Fragaria virginiana*)	6 inches	Dry to moist	Sun to shade	3-8	✔			Blooms April-June followed by fruit.	All regions
American Black Elderberry (*Sambucus canadensis*)	9 to 12 feet tall	Prefers rich, moist	Sun to partial shade	3-9	✔		✔	Clusters of white flowers in spring. Purple-black drupe in late summer to early fall.	Northeast
Pilgrim Cranberry (*Vaccinium macrocarpon* 'Pilgrim')	6 to 12 inches tall and 18 to 24 inches wide	Moist, well-drained soil	Sun to partial shade	4-8	✔			White to pink flowers in May followed by dark red tart fruit.	Northeast, Midwest
Lowbush Blueberry (*Vaccinium angustifolium*)	6 inches to 2 feet tall	Dry to moist soil	Full sun to shade	2-8	✔			Fruits in July-August.	Northeast, some Midwest
Highbush Cranberry (*Viburnum opulus* var. *americanum*)	8 to 10 feet (height and spread)	Moist soil and good drainage	Full sun to part shade	2-7	✔			White flowers in spring. Bright red fruit in fall that last through winter.	Northeast, some Midwest
Black Chokeberry (*Aronia melanocarpa*)	3 to 5 feet (height and spread)	Water infrequently but thoroughly	Full sun to part shade	3-8	✔			White flowers in spring. Berries form by autumn, and stay on shrub throughout winter.	Northeast, partial Midwest

ADDITIONAL OPTIONS BASED ON YOUR REGION

Plant name	Plant size	Water needs	Preferred lighting conditions	Hardy to (USDA zones)	Provides ✿	🌲🌲	🪺	Main season of interest	Native range
Serviceberry (*Amerlanchier* spp.)	10 to 25 feet tall	Well-drained soil	Full sun to partial shade	4-9	✓			One of the first to flower in the spring with white blossoms that later produce fruit.	Northeast, some Southeast, some Southwest
Blackberries (*Rubus* spp.)	3 to 6 feet tall	Rich, fertile soil	Light shade to full sun	3-10	✓	✓		Berries are produced early in the growing season. Can spread aggressively but easier to control in raised beds. Supporting the canes with trellising is recommended.	Northeast
Black Raspberry (*Rubus occidentalis*)	3 to 5 feet tall and wide	Dry, moist, gravelly soils	Full sun to shade	5-8	✓			Fruit in late summer. Supporting the canes with trellising is recommended.	Northeast
Choke Cherry (*Prunus virginiana*)	20 to 30 feet tall	Moist, well-drained loam	Full sun to part shade	2-7	✓			Cherries ripen in July and August. Feeds songbirds and other mammals. **Note: fruit not edible for humans.**	Midwest, Southeast
Winterberry (*Ilex verticillata*)	6 to 15 feet tall	Dry to wet soil	Full sun to shade	3-9	✓			Red berries over winter. ***Need at least one male plant to pollinate female plants to get the berries.**	Southeast, Northeast

Susie Creamer

Susie Creamer works to create more bird-friendly habitats in Maryland.

⚲ BALTIMORE, MARYLAND

Susie Creamer first noticed the birds around her when she was floating in a dugout canoe in a Bolivian tributary of the Amazon River. Susie just finished her service as an environmental education Peace Corps Volunteer in Paraguay. "I was watching Scarlet Macaws feed in the morning light," she explains. "The abundance of so many brightly colored birds that morning and throughout our journey in the rainforest enlightened me to the wonder of birds."

These days, she doesn't need to travel to the Amazon to be amazed by the variety and diversity of migrating songbirds that cross the American continents. In spring, Susie looks forward to the colorful warblers that will stop through for a brief visit on their way to the breeding grounds.

"I am repeatedly humbled by the incredible feat of migration and what so many small birds accomplish despite countless obstacles," she said. "It seems many people overlook migration and the need for birds to have adequate resources along their migratory paths."

Susie is the Center Director for Patterson Park Audubon Center in Baltimore, Maryland. She and her colleagues offer educational presentations on gardening for birds, lead habitat restoration projects in the city, and collaborate with a number of partner organizations to ensure that the plants included in the Baltimore Center plans are the best species to support the birds.

"I focus on improving our city for birds and our communities," she said. "Often that means transforming neglected spaces into flowering gardens that beautify neighborhoods while providing food, shelter, and nesting materials for birds."

The green spaces can be large, forested city parks of small patches of land "with an ounce of refuge."

"I continue to be amazed when migrants will stop by urban patches of green during their journeys," she said. There are many opportunities for ecosystem restoration in the city, and creative ways to make it attractive to people as well.

"Working in dense Baltimore City neighborhoods, I like to flip the narrative that you have to get out of the city to experience nature. Despite habitat fragmentation and invasive species, there is plenty of nature to explore within the city. Though we still need more biodiversity in urban areas, birds are already showing us that our efforts are worth it."

To help the resident and migrating songbirds in the area, Susie includes native species that offer fruit, nectar, seeds, and insects in her garden spaces for the birds to eat. She creates layers of cover with ground covers, shrubs, and trees to provide shelter and nesting areas. She offers fresh water and avoids using chemicals in the garden. Susie's favorite native plant combination is Black-eyed Susan (*Rudbeckia hirta*) and Purple Coneflower (*Echinacea purpurea*). "They look beautiful together, and both are popular for the seeds they provide. I see tons of goldfinches on them in summer."

Susie and her team help others in the community see the meaningful connections between birds and people, with the goal of encouraging more residents to create bird-friendly habitats on their property. This can include front and side yards, and even patio gardens. The team also led trainings for the city's housing inspectors on identifying native plants and recognizing "wild-scaped" gardens as opposed to blighted properties.

Susie attributes birding to recognizing the interconnectedness of people across the Americas. "Working in partnership with Baltimore's Latino community, I appreciate how birds connect people across borders and travel without passports to find safe places to raise their young," she said. "People share these needs and are often inspired by the close connection they share with migratory birds. We have a lot to learn from nature, and birds remind me to observe and appreciate their teachings."

In collaboration with community leaders and partner organizations, Patterson Park Audubon Center designed and created the Mural Garden of Library Square, a transformation project to convert a vacant lot, filled with rubble from a building demolition, into a warm welcome to southeast Baltimore City, Maryland, where it invites birds and people to enjoy its benefits.

Native plant rain garden

Our world includes many impermeable surfaces where water cannot be absorbed, such as parking lots, flat rooftops, driveways, and sidewalks.

Recent scientific studies have found that with the increase in the earth's temperature (due to climate change), the warm air is able to "hold" more water. A 2022 study found that rainfall has increased in the United States in recent decades, and in some regions of the U.S., the intensity of the rainfall has shifted from lighter to more moderate to heavy deluges. This was found most in areas east of the Rocky Mountains (with an increase of about 5 percent more precipitation). For rainfall over the Pacific Coast or Rocky Mountains, rainfall intensity changes were not observed (Harp & Horton).

The hotter it is, the more water that will evaporate into the air. When it storms, the warmer air is more likely to unleash heavy rain as opposed to light rain. According to the U.S. Environmental Protection Agency, "heavy precipitation does not mean the total amount of precipitation at a location has increased—just that precipitation is occurring in more intense events" (2021).

Where does all the excess rain go? Lots of rain in a short amount of time, especially in areas with lots of paved surfaces, can quickly overwhelm storm drains. All that water has to go somewhere because it isn't being absorbed into the ground.

One way gardeners can help counteract flooding is to equip properties so they are able to hold and absorb more water over a longer period of time. One way to help slow down water is to install rain gardens on properties that are adjacent to paved surfaces, such as driveways. Rain gardens are also great landscape features to incorporate into urban landscapes, where pavement abounds.

Rain gardens are shallow depressions (usually bowl-shaped) and feature plants that can tolerate water fluctuation—and help the earth slowly absorb the water back into the soil. A rain garden can help

A Northern Mockingbird scouts from a tall tree.

hold water during a torrential storm, instead of the excess water overwhelming sewage systems and streams. Rain gardens can even help with melting snow in colder months.

Rain gardens are also pretty powerful when it comes to keeping nature healthy. The storm water runoff that collects in the rain gardens prevents it from flowing directly into lakes, rivers, and wetlands. As the water is slowly absorbed back into the soil, it is also filtered by the soil, removing pollutants from entering groundwater. Native plants used in rain gardens can also help prevent erosion due to the plant roots and their holding ability.

Fact or fiction?

Ⓠ Will I have lots of mosquitoes if I have a rain garden?

Ⓐ No. According to Penn State Extension, mosquitoes require at least seven days of standing water to complete their egg laying and hatching cycle.

Ⓠ I have a pond or a wetland area on my property. Does that count as a rain garden?

Ⓐ No. Rain gardens temporarily hold rainwater so it can soak into the soil between 24-48 hours afterward. Rain gardens are actually dry most of the time—they only hold water after a rain storm.

Ⓠ Can I use any type of plant in a rain garden?

Ⓐ The ideal plants for a rain garden are native varieties that do not mind brief periods of excess water and can also tolerate some portions of drought. These can include perennials or shrubs, and can be beneficial to insects and birds.

Ⓠ I'm unsure of the best place to set up a rain garden. Who can I ask for help?

Ⓐ Reach out to your state's cooperative extension service, which will have local experts who can help.

Rose Mallow (*Hibiscus moscheutos*) is a perennial flower that blooms in the summer. The flowers last for about a day. This plant works in the "wet zone" portion of a rain garden.

Black Chokeberry (*Aronia melanocarpa*) is one small tree that works well in a rain garden setting.

A rain garden can be installed near a gutter downspout to help divert excess water (as opposed to the gutters releasing rainwater on paved surfaces). But rain gardens are not just areas of standing water on a property. A properly situated rain garden is created in a spot with well-draining soil. (Compacted soil will often create areas of standing water.) The water in a rain garden needs to be absorbed ideally within 24 hours after a storm, and completely within 48 hours to prevent plant roots from rotting.

BUILDING THE RAIN GARDEN

Most residential rain gardens range in size from 100 to 300 square feet, and are about 4 to 8 inches deep. They are best suited for areas of full sun to part sun, and should not be located directly under a tree canopy.

For the rain garden to work properly, one side slopes downward (where the water will temporarily collect). There are three main zones of the rain garden: the wet zone, the middle zone, and the transition zone.

- **Wet zone** This area will hold the water the longest, and is the deepest part of the rain garden. Supplemental water may be necessary for the wet zone plants if they are experiencing drought conditions.
- **Middle zone** The soil in this area drains more quickly than the wet zone.
- **Transition zone** This is the portion of the rain garden that will dry out first (it is the shallowest part of the rain garden).

The rain garden will also need a berm on one side to prevent soil from washing away. A berm in a rain garden is a raised portion of land, usually created with the soil that was removed for the wet zone (deeper portion) of the rain garden.

BIRDS ATTRACTED

 Finches

 Hummingbirds

 Nuthatches

 Crows, Magpies & Jays

 Thrushes

 Chickadees & Titmice

 Wood Warblers

 Wrens

 New World Sparrows

 Waxwings

 Woodpeckers

 Vireos

 Mockingbirds & Thrashers

 Cardinals, Grosbeaks & Buntings

 Blackbirds & Orioles

Customize

Rain gardens can easily be customized to your available outdoor space as well. Even though they are highly adaptable, there are placement pointers to keep in mind:

Numbers to remember

- **10**—Keep rain gardens away from house foundations (10 feet or more) to prevent water issues in basements.
- **35**—Keep rain gardens away from septic system drain fields (35 feet or more).
- **50**—Keep rain gardens away from drinking water wells and utility lines (50 feet or more).

A juvenile Cedar Waxwing perched on a branch.

PLANTS FEATURED IN ILLUSTRATION:

Ⓐ Mistflower
(*Eupatorium coelestinum*)

Ⓑ Black chokeberry
(*Aronia melanocarpa*)

Ⓒ Witch hazel
(*Hammamelis virginiana*)

Ⓓ Swamp sunflower
(*Helianthus angustifolius*)

Ⓔ White Turtlehead
(*Chelone glabra*),

Ⓕ Swamp milkweed
(*Asclepias incarnata*)

Ⓖ Rose mallow
(*Hibiscus moscheutos*)

THIS NATIVE PLANT RAIN GARDEN FEATURES THE FOLLOWING NATIVE PLANTS

Plant name	Plant size	Water needs	Preferred lighting conditions	Hardy to (USDA zones)	Provides			Main season of interest	Native range
White Turtlehead (*Chelone glabra*)	24 to 36 inches tall and 18 to 24 inches wide	Moist to wet soil	Part sun	3-8	✓		✓	Provides nesting material for birds. Flowers attract hummingbirds.	Southeast, Northeast, partial Midwest
Rose Mallow (*Hibiscus moscheutos*)	3 to 6 feet tall and 2 to 3 feet wide	Wet to constantly moist	Part sun to full sun	5-9	✓		✓	Pink or white flowers that bloom summer through early fall. Birds will eat seeds in fall and winter.	Northeast, Southeast, South
Swamp Sunflower (*Helianthus angustifolius*)	3 to 10 feet tall and 2 to 4 feet wide	Moist to wet	Sun	5-9	✓			Maturing seedheads will feed birds. Plants will spread so start with one.	Southeast, partial Northeast, and partial Southwest
Swamp Milkweed (*Asclepias incarnata*)	3 to 5 feet tall and 1 to 2 feet wide	Moist, medium to wet clay soil.	Part sun to sun	3-9	✓			Flowers will attract hummingbirds. Also host plant for monarch butterflies.	Southeast, parts of Northeast, Southwest and Midwest
Black Chokeberry (*Aronia melanocarpa*)	3 to 5 feet (height and spread)	Water infrequently but thoroughly.	Full sun to part shade	3-8	✓			White flowers in spring. Berries form by autumn and stay on shrub throughout winter.	Northeast, partial Midwest
Witch Hazel (*Hamamelis virginiana*)	15 to 20 feet tall and wide	Average soil moisture	Sun to part shade	3-8	✓		✓	Flowers in late fall. Birds eat the seeds after they fall to the ground. Upright branches are ideal nesting sites.	Northeast, Southeast
Mistflower (*Conoclinium coelestinum*)	1 to 3 feet tall and up to 2 feet wide	Moist	Sun to part shade	5-9	✓			Many insects are attracted to the flowers of this plant, including butterflies.	Southeast, some Southwest, partial Northeast, partial Midwest

ALSO CONSIDER THE FOLLOWING OPTIONS

Plant name	Plant size	Water needs	Preferred lighting conditions	Hardy to (USDA zones)	Provides 🌸 🌲 🪺			Main season of interest	Native range
Bayberry (*Morella pensylvanica*)	5 to 8 feet tall	Adaptable to sandy or clay soils	Full to part sun	2-9	✓	✓		Berries attract birds and will provide shelter for birds when grown as a hedge.	Northeast, Southeast
Cardinal Flower (*Lobelia cardinalis*)	1 to 6 feet tall	Moist	Sun to part shade	2-8	✓			Flowers are specialized for feeding hummingbirds.	Northeast, Southwest, Midwest, and some Southwest
Blue flag Iris (*Iris versicolor*)	Up to 30 inches tall and 1 to 2 inches wide	Moist to wet	Sunny	2-7	✓			Flowers are attractive to hummingbirds.	Northeast, some Midwest, some West
Top Point Atlantic White Cedar (*Chamaecyparis thyoides* 'Top Point')	4 to 5 feet tall and 2 to 3 feet wide	Average, well-drained soil	Full sun	4-8	✓	✓		Berries in fall. Winter color in the landscape.	Northeast, Southeast
Winterberry (*Ilex verticillata*)	6 to 15 feet tall	Dry to wet soil	Full sun to shade	3-9	✓			Red berries over winter. ***Need at least one male plant to pollinate female plants for fruit.**	Southeast, Northeast
Spicebush (*Lindera benzoin*)	4 to 12 feet high and wide	Wet to well-drained, but can tolerate dry	Part shade to part sun	4-9	✓	✓		Both female and male plants are needed to produce berries.	Northeast, Southeast, partial West
Virginia Sweetspire (*Itea virginica*)	3 to 6 feet tall and 4 to 5 feet wide	Dry to moist (Tolerant of boggy to dry soils)	Sun to part shade	5-9	✓	✓		Cultivars will stay more compact. Fragrant white blooms in late spring attract pollinators and seeds feed birds.	Northeast, Southeast, some Southwest

Incorporating bird feeders into your garden

Bird-friendly habitats contain a variety of food for birds to eat: larvae to feed their young, berries to relish, and seeds to devour. But using bird feeders to provide supplemental food—seed, suet, fruit, or nectar—along with the native plants your garden offers is an additional way to entice birds to the garden. Not all birds will visit feeders—many warblers for example prefer to hunt for insects in the layers of shrubs and trees. But many do, such as Bullock's Orioles, Northern Cardinals, House Finches, Tufted Titmice, and Black-capped Chickadees.

Providing birdseed in the fall and winter months also provides birds such as chickadees, nuthatches, jays, woodpeckers, and crows the ability to "cache" food, or store it for use later in the season. According to The Cornell Lab of Ornithology, many species will remember the hiding spots and even what type of food they hid there. If it seems that another animal or bird has been poking around and may have seen where the food was stashed, the bird may re-hide the seeds for safekeeping.

During harsh winter weather, supplemental seed and suet can benefit birds who may not be able to access their cached food or overwintering insects. And in the warmer months, hummingbird feeders can provide an additional calorie perk for birds migrating through at the end or beginning of the season. This

A Tufted Titmouse perches in a tree after retrieving a black-oil sunflower seed from a nearby bird feeder.

is especially helpful if the garden's season of bloom—or perhaps more accurately described as season of food—is still a work in progress.

Bird feeders can also help other individuals develop an appreciation for birds. School classrooms can mount bird feeders to windows (usually with suction cups), providing an opportunity for children to observe wild birds closely but safely. There are also many new feeders that are able to take photos or short videos of the birds that visit. This media can then be shared with family and friends.

Bird feeding does serve as a great introduction to helping individuals connect with birds, and as people learn more about the birds visiting their gardens and private spaces, the more likely they will want to further improve the property with more native plant offerings and incorporate nature-friendly designs into their properties.

No matter which bird feeder you decide to add to complement your garden's offerings, the most important part is making sure the feeders are cleaned regularly to prevent moldy food from accumulating (either seed, syrup, or suet) or diseases from spreading. For example, hummingbird feeders that provide sugar water nectar but are not regularly cleaned and refreshed can do more harm than good. A hummingbird's tongue can swell from the bacteria in the expired sugar water, and can ultimately cause death. (See page 29 for safe feeder practices.)

If regularly cleaning feeders is not a possibility—either due to schedules or accessibility—then it is better not to use bird feeders at all. But if keeping feeders clean and filled with food is an activity you can commit to, then read on.

THE LONG HISTORY OF BIRD FEEDING

The earliest records of Americans feeding birds are sourced back to the late nineteenth century—which also coincides with the bird protection movement. Tips to attract the birds included nailing suet to trees and putting out "winter-feeding shelves" filled with seeds or table scraps. By the 1920s, farmers were advised to feed birds during winter months to encourage the birds to stay during the warmer season to eat weed seeds and insects. Quite simply, birds were advertised as allies to help protect crops (Baicich, Barker, and Henderson 2015).

Jump ahead to the 1950s, when people began to focus on using certain varieties of seed to attract birds to feeders—such as sunflower seeds, safflower seeds, and peanuts. Previously, most birdseed mixes at stores contained what we now call **filler seeds**—cracked corn, millet, and milo. By the 1980s and 1990s, more specialized bird feeders and seed became more easily available to purchase, especially at specialty wild bird shops and garden centers. Many more people realized that bird feeders provided an additional opportunity for attracting birds to private property for observation and enjoyment.

A Blue Jay inspects an acorn from an oak tree.

A Black-capped Chickadee takes a seed from a bird feeder to cache for future use.

Below are different types of bird feeders that you can set up in your garden space. Remember, if any seed becomes soggy or grows mold, discard it.

- **Mealworm feeder** These feeders can hold either dried or live meal worms to feed insectivorous birds such as the Eastern Bluebird. However, House Sparrows and European Starlings can become pests when they find out this food is available, and will often swarm the feeders and make it impossible for other birds to approach. Placing the feeder inside a wire guard will keep out starlings, and setting this feeder up away from other seed feeders that House Sparrows may visit will help minimize their visits.

- **Suet feeder** Suet feeders will attract woodpeckers to your garden space, such as Red-Headed Woodpeckers and Downy Woodpeckers, along with other small songbirds, such as Mountain Chickadees, Bushtits, and Oak Titmice. Often supplied in the colder season as a source of fat reserves for birds, suet can also be placed out in the summer as long as it is a no-melt variety. For days when the temperature is 85°F to 90°F or higher, omit suet from the food offerings to prevent suet from turning rancid.

- **Seed hopper feeders** These feeders often have a central repository for seed that allows seed to be dispersed into a tray. It is usually covered with a roof, which protects the unused seed from the weather. The platform area aligning along the tray provides more space for birds to perch while eating. Sunflower seeds are a popular choice for this style of feeder, attracting Jays and Tufted Titmice.

- **Platform feeders** These open tray feeders can be mounted on small feet and placed at ground level to attract ground-feeding birds, such as Mourning Doves, White-throated Sparrows, towhees, thrashers, and Dark-eyed Juncos. Or they can be mounted to a pole to offer food in a higher spot, attracting species such as Cactus Wrens, nuthatches, jays, and titmice. These trays need to be cleaned regularly since the seed is not protected from the weather.

Two Eastern Bluebirds feed from a mealworm feeder, while a Northern Cardinal clings outside on the wire guard.

Downy Woodpeckers will regularly visit suet feeders.

- **Seed tube feeders** Usually a hanging feeder, these tubular style feeders have perches along the length of the feeder for small birds to perch on while eating. These are attractive to Pine Siskins and finches.

- **Nyjer feeder or finch feeders** These skinny, tubular feeders have small perches that goldfinches can easily perch on to feed, but they are too small for larger birds. While this is very attractive to finches, the nyjer seed that is often used to fill it is imported. It is also referred to as a thistle feeder.

- **Peanut feeders** These feeders come in a variety of shapes to hold peanuts for birds to pluck from the mesh openings in the feeder. They can either hold shells or peanuts in the shell, and are attractive to jays and woodpeckers.

- **Sugar water feeders** This style of feeder is primarily used during warmer seasons to provide supplemental food for hummingbirds, but Bullock Orioles also feed on nectar and from sugar-water feeders. To attract hummingbirds to a new feeder, place it near blooming flowers early in the season. Once a hummingbird knows supplemental food will be supplied, it will return to the spot each year. You can also set feeders up on balconies, patios, and by windows to get a closer view of the birds. Depending on how many hummingbirds visit the property, you can use several small feeders or a few larger ones. (Ruby-throated Hummingbirds are territorial, so the videos of seeing numerous hummingbirds feeding at once are often western species.)

- **Fruit feeders** These feeders feature prongs to hold slices of oranges or dishes filled with grape jelly to lure orioles, tanagers, and Gray Catbirds. Sliced apples can be offered to entice bluebirds. Raisins and currants can be added to attract waxwings and mockingbirds—either in the feeder or mixed in with a platform feeder's offerings.

A variety of birds will visit feeders in the garden.

A male Baltimore Oriole feeds on grape jelly at this specialized feeder.

IDEAL PLACEMENT IS KEY TO ATTRACT VISITORS

With all these feeders to choose from, putting out supplemental food should be easy, right? The next important step is choosing the safest place to mount the feeder. Look for an area that provides a natural windbreak for birds to shelter in during inclement weather. The feeder should be placed 10 feet away from any neighboring tree or shrub to prevent squirrels, chipmunks, and mice from stealing food.

A squirrel guard or baffle (at least 17 inches in diameter) mounted on the pole will help keep squirrels off feeders. This prevents squirrels from being able to climb up the pole to the seed. To avoid window strikes (see page 40), it is recommended to place your feeders within three feet of windows that may reflect the surrounding landscape.

Choose an area that does not have many plants growing underneath. The area underneath a feeder will become a high traffic area with area wildlife, so plants located directly beneath the feeder can be damaged in the process. Placing the feeder on the edge of a garden bed will be more beneficial than right in the middle of a flower bed.

Periodically sweeping up spilled seed and seed hulls will also help keep the area clean, and discourage rodents from gathering underneath to eat spilled seed. Another reason to remove discarded seed hulls is that sunflower seed hulls can actually inhibit other plants from germinating, which can affect a groundcover or grass below the feeder.

Birds may not frequent a feeder that is placed in the middle of a lawn as much as a feeder mounted closer to trees and shrubs. The latter provides cover to escape into if the birds feel threatened by predators—either cats or hawks.

Offering an assortment of feeders at varying heights will help attract more bird species to the garden, and help minimize competition at one feeder. These can be spaced out to prevent overcrowding in one area.

A pair of Tufted Titmice visit a seed hopper feeder.

Although there are a variety of bird feeders on the market, many birds will find native plants and their seeds desirable food options.

Ways to reduce your lawn area

Many U.S. properties have one feature in common—they include a sizeable chunk of lawn that surrounds the home. All those front and back lawns add up. It's estimated that lawn covers 50 million acres in the U.S. Of that, 31 million acres are regularly irrigated. That's a lot of water to use on a plant that offers very little ecological benefit to wildlife! Songbirds, native insects, and other wildlife will often pass through a large expanse of lawn in an effort to find food and suitable nesting areas. To encourage birds to stay on the property, homeowners can incorporate native plants and garden spaces to break up the green grass. Plus, saving water from watering lawns and other non-native plants will save you money.

According to the U.S. Environmental Protection Agency, the average U.S. household uses more water outdoors than for showering and washing clothes combined; residential outdoor water use adds up to 8 billion gallons of water a day—mainly for landscape irrigation. Despite all the additional water needed to keep lawns green, lawns have less than 10 percent of the water absorbing capacity of natural woodlands, which can contribute to flooding in suburban areas.

Grasses that make up lawns do not grow tall enough to provide cover for birds, as many native grasses used in landscaping plans do. Lawns that receive regular applications of chemical fertilizers and pesticides are often devoid of life—further contributing to the monoculture desert that

A green lawn is a common sight across many American gardens, even in late fall with a light frost! Green lawns typically require significant irrigation, application of fertilizer or pesticides, and care to maintain.

stretches across property borders. Mowers and other gas-powered lawn equipment used for keeping the grass blades at a desirable (short) height often release harmful emissions into the atmosphere.

No matter the size commitment, removing a portion of the lawn for native plantings will make a big difference for birds. Converting a dedicated lawn area over to a native plant garden can be done gradually over time, beginning with one garden bed, and slowly expanding it over the years. Or large portions of a lawn can be removed and replanted with native plants in one season.

Another option to consider—which includes less labor—is to not mow, fertilize, or water the lawn. Allowing a lawn to grow on its own without maintenance will create cover and potentially more insect life. For a slightly less wild look, a path can be mown into the free-growing grass. An added benefit of longer grass is that it is better at retaining moisture, so it will be less prone to drought in drier weather. Grass kept long over the winter will also provide shelter and habitat to a variety of insects, which can also provide food for birds (Hardy 2015).

LAYERING WITH CARDBOARD

One of the easier ways to begin a new garden bed involves layering pieces of cardboard over existing grass. This practice is also referred to as "sheet mulching." Compost, leaf mulch, or shredded mulch is added on top of the cardboard to contribute to the enzymes in the soil that help to break it down. Deprived of sunlight, the grass underneath will eventually die—and the cardboard will also break down over time. This process works best on a flat area of the garden.

When layering the carboard pieces, overlap the pieces so grass cannot escape through the gaps. After applying the cardboard layer, water well to help the decomposition process.

This technique works well in the spring or the fall. In the fall, the grass can break down when the garden is in the "off season." Cardboard laid down in the spring will benefit from the summer heat aiding the decomposition process. The cardboard—with the organic matter on top—should be left in place for

at least 6 to 8 weeks to allow the grass underneath to die and begin to decompose. Then you can start planting. Keep an eye out for rogue weeds as your native plants grow, and remove as necessary. Using a mulch after planting will also help keep weeds in check.

REMOVING TURF WITH A SHOVEL

Another option to remove grass is by slicing it in chunks (6 inches × 12 inches) and removing it for immediate planting. Shake off the excess soil from the grass roots before removing and putting in the compost pile. New compost and soil can be brought in and laid on top of the exposed garden soil.

One way to create new garden beds is to mark the lawn and remove it in chunks with a shovel.

If the bed will be sitting dormant for a period of time, you can turn the chunks of grass upside down with the roots exposed to air and sunlight. As the plants die, they will decompose and can be worked back into the soil.

CONNECTING FUTURE GARDEN BEDS

Garden beds can be added gradually to a lawn area and later connected by a path that further cuts through the grassy area. Using shredded mulch or a permeable material—such as pea gravel—will help excess water from heavy rainfall absorb into the ground. Stone or concrete pavers can also be used and placed on top of the mulch or pea gravel, as opposed to making one continuous stone path that is cemented together.

CONSIDER NATIVE GROUNDCOVERS

Native groundcovers offer another way to provide plant variety to a garden space, and work well in areas where grass may have a difficult time growing (such as shady areas). Many groundcovers will remain low to the ground and will help cover bare soil to prevent weeds from sprouting. Plants such as American Cranberry (*Vaccinium macrocarpon*) can grow in moist, full sun areas and Appalachian Sedge (*Carex appalachica*) in dry, shady locations.

Removing areas of lawn with a shovel will provide immediate access for planting. Top dress the area with compost to provide an organic boost for transplanted plants.

In this photo, a town park created a raised bed for native plants. This area was once covered only in grass.

Replace your lawn with a collection of plants native to your region.

Hummingbird haven/balcony patio garden

Drawing hummingbirds closer to a balcony or patio garden can be easily done when you plan for them. Some hummingbirds, such as the Ruby-throated Hummingbird, will migrate through the North American east coast during the prime breeding season. Hummingbirds that are found west of the Rocky Mountains, such as Allen's and Rufous Hummingbirds, also migrate but can also be year-round residents in certain areas.

Hummingbirds

Did you know? There are fifteen hummingbird species that regularly breed in the United States. Seven of these species remain in the deep Southwest or Texas. The other eight species are more geographically widespread and include Allen's Hummingbird, Anna's Hummingbird, Black-chinned Hummingbird, Broad-tailed Hummingbird, Calliope Hummingbird, Costa's Hummingbird, Ruby-throated Hummingbird, and the Rufous Hummingbird (Source: Shewey 2021).

To create a viable hummingbird habitat for a balcony or patio garden, there should be a plethora of nectar-rich plants that will bloom throughout the season. Many of the plants that are attractive to hummingbirds—and have evolved to cater to hummingbirds for pollination—will be brightly colored but low on fragrance (since birds are attracted to flowers by vision), and are often tubular in form in order for a hummingbird's bill and tongue to reach the nectar.

Silene virginica and *Agastache* spp. are two flowering plants that can be planted together in a window box to attract hummingbirds.

Broad-tailed Hummingbird from the Western U.S.

When given the proper size container and preferred soil mixture, many native plants will grow well in containers, either individually or grouped with other varieties. When choosing a container, look for one that will fit your space—either displayed on an outdoor table, mounted underneath a window, or secured on a balcony railing. Large containers can be placed in corners of the balcony or patio, and can be placed on wheeled trays before filling with soil and plants to make moving easier in the future.

One western species to try in a container is Canyon Delphinium (*Delphinium nudicaule*), which features scarlet red flowers in spring and does well in partly shady areas. (Keep away from pets and children—the plant is toxic if ingested.)

Offering a nectar feeder will also entice hummingbirds to visit and provide food during any seasonal gaps when plants are not in bloom, or complement the ever-blooming habitat. (See page 29 for information on hummingbird feeders.)

Adding a water mister to a small birdbath (or a bubbler water fountain) as an additional feature will also entice hummingbirds to visit. The smaller water feature can be grouped with the mixed container plantings or in an open area.

A window box makes a perfect home for a variety of native plants throughout the seasons. This window box project used one Red Columbine, one Fire Pink and two compact varieties of Anise Hyssop. The window box was sized 11 inches high × 36 inches wide × 11 inches deep and was a self-watering plastic box.

The featured plants in the charts on the following page are native to the continental United States and are attractive to hummingbirds (and a few other birds will show up for the seeds later in the season).

BIRDS ATTRACTED

 Hummingbirds

 Finches

 New World Sparrows

Wild Bergamot (*Monarda fistulosa*) is a perennial that will grow in a large container.

A window box filled with late-season flowers is perched on top of a fence bordering suburban properties.

NATIVE PLANT WINDOW BOX GARDEN

The following native plants can also be mixed and matched in container plantings. When combining plants, group plants with similar water and lighting needs together. Plants can also be potted up individually.

Plant name	Plant size	Water needs	Preferred lighting conditions	Hardy to (USDA zones)	Provides			Main season of interest	Native range
					✿	🌲	🪹		
Red Columbine (*Aquilegia canadensis*)	3 to 4 feet tall and about 1 foot wide	Dry, well-drained soil	Partial to full shade	3-8	✓			Red and yellow flowers attract hummingbirds in spring. Finches eat seeds.	Northeast, Southeast, part Midwest
Fire Pink (*Silene virginica*)	1 to 3 feet	Moist, well-drained sandy or clay soil	Full sun to part shade	4-8	✓			Red blooms in late spring attract Ruby-throated Hummingbirds. A short-lived perennial. Seeds will attract juncos, Pine Siskins, and sparrows.	Northeast, Southeast, partial Midwest
Anise Hyssop (*Agastache foeniculum*)	2 to 4 feet	Dry to average soil. Well-drained.	Sun to part shade	5-9	✓			Compact varieties which feature purple flowers in summer attract hummingbirds. Finches will eat the seeds.	Midwest

How to make a large container less heavy (and easier to move)

Tall and large containers help add dramatic focal points to balcony and patio garden, especially when grouped with other containers of various sizes. These large containers will hold more soil, which in turn will add to the weight of the planter. One way to make larger pots easier to move around is to add a layer of filler material to the bottom of the container. This will replace some of the soil that is used to fill the pot.

One way to repurpose disposable plastic bottles is by adding them in a layer at the bottom of a taller container (up to one third of the bottom of the planter can be filled this way). The potting soil mixture can then be added on top of the bottles. Plant the container with annuals or short-lived perennials. Make sure there is a drainage hole at the bottom of all containers to allow excess water to drain away.

ALSO CONSIDER THE FOLLOWING OPTIONS

Plant name	Plant size	Water needs	Preferred lighting conditions	Hardy to (USDA zones)	Provides ✿ 🌲 🪹			Main season of interest	Native range
Indian Pink (*Spigelia marilandica*)	1 to 2 feet and up to 1.5 feet wide	Average to moist, well-drained soil	Part to full shade	5-9	✓			Red and yellow flowers are a great source of nectar for hummingbirds.	Southeast, partial Southwest
Wild Bergamot (*Monarda fistulosa*)	3 to 4 feet tall	Dry to moist, well-draining soil.	Full sun to partial shade	3a-8b	✓			Lavender flowers from June through August that attract hummingbirds.	West
Butterfly Milkweed (*Asclepias tuberosa*)	1 to 3 feet tall	Dry to moist soil	Full sun	3-9	✓			Host plant for butterfly species such as the monarch. Hummingbirds will feed from orange flowers.	Northeast, Southeast, Midwest, partial Southwest
Wild Canterbury Bells (*Phacelia minor*)	8 to 24 inches tall	Little water	Full sun	5-10	✓			Annual herb which produces blue to purple bell-shaped flowers.	West
Western Red Columbine (*Aquilegia formosa*)	18 to 36 inches tall	Well-drained soil	Full sun to part shade	3-9	✓			Red and yellow blooms in late spring to early summer. Short-lived perennial.	West
Firecracker Penstemon (*Penstemon eatonii*)	2.5 to 3 feet tall and 15 inches wide	Lean, well-drained soil	Full sun to part shade	4-8	✓			Red flowers are attractive to hummingbirds.	West
Wild Four O'Clock (*Mirabilis* spp.)	15 to 18 inches tall and 48 to 72 inches wide	Lean soil	Full sun	4-8	✓			Magenta pink flowers bloom in the afternoon during the summer. ***Limit watering to encourage blooms, not leaves.**	West, Southwest
Royal Catchfly (*Silene regia*)	24 to 48 inches tall and 15 inches wide	Rich, well-drained sandy or loam soils	Full sun	4-9	✓			Scarlet-red flowers attract hummingbirds.	Midwest
Canyon Delphinium (*Delphinium nudicaule*)	1 to 2 feet tall and wide	Well-drained, moist to dry soil	Part shade	7-9	✓			Hummingbirds will feed from the early blooms.	West

Shady patio retreat

Small patio areas that are shaded offer intimate pockets of habitat for birds. Native plants that perform well in moist soil will do best in this shady spot, and adding a small birdbath with a bubbler can help further the peaceful vibes, and attract birds to the moving water sounds as well.

Many of the plants featured for a shady patio retreat are very attractive to hummingbirds, such as the red-tipped flowers of Indian Pink (*Spigelia marilandica*), the bell-shaped flowers of Coral Bells (*Heuchera villosa*), and the early blooming pink flowers of Fringed Bleeding Heart (*Dicentra eximia*). At least one of each of these should be considered for use in a small space—multiples of three would be even better if space permits.

Adding at least one Cinnamon Fern (*Osmunda cinnamomeum*) will provide a dramatic backdrop for the garden. An early season grower, Jack-in-the-Pulpit (*Arisaema triphyllum*) can be interplanted with Red Columbine (*Aquilegia canadensis*). Golden Alexander (*Zizia aurea*), the native host plant for the Black Swallowtail Butterfly, will also attract other beneficial insects to the garden as well.

If a trellis or wall is adjacent to the shady patio area, consider adding Virginia Creeper (*Parthenocissus quinquefolia*) to the plan. It will spread up a wall or even act as a groundcover and is easy to cut back if it gets a little too greedy for space. As this plant matures, it will produce blue berries that are attractive to chickadees, nuthatches, mockingbirds, catbirds, finches, flycatchers, tanagers, swallows, vireos, warblers, woodpeckers, and thrushes. (The berries are toxic to humans though.) This native vine is sometimes confused with another unpopular native plant, poison ivy. (Keep in mind the rhyme when in doubt: **Leaves of three, let it be; Leaves of five, let it thrive**.)

Cinnamon Fern (*Osmunda cinnamomeum*) is a native plant that prefers moist soil. In early spring, the fiddleheads produce a fuzz that birds will use as a nesting material.

Red Columbine (*Aquilegia canadensis*) is an early blooming perennial that stays fairly compact and grows well in a shady garden area.

Golden Alexander (*Zizia aurea*) grows well in sun to part shade.

Purple Turtlehead (*Chelone obliqua*) bloom from July through August. The flowers are attractive to hummingbirds.

BIRDS ATTRACTED

 Wood Warblers

 Blackbirds & Orioles

 Crows, Magpies & Jays

 New World Sparrows

 Vireos

 Wrens

 Finches

 Thrushes

 Cardinals, Grosbeaks & Buntings

 Woodpeckers

 Waxwings

 Mockingbirds & Thrashers

 Chickadees & Titmice

 Nuthatches

 Hummingbirds

An American Robin perches on top of a garage roof where Virginia Creeper (*Parthenocissus quinquefolia*) is allowed to grow.

A female Northern Cardinal perches on top of a garden statue.

THIS SHADY PATIO RETREAT FEATURES THE FOLLOWING NATIVE PLANTS

Plant name	Plant size	Water needs	Preferred lighting conditions	Hardy to (USDA zones)	Provides			Main season of interest	Native range
					✿	▲▲	⬤		
Wild Geranium (*Geranium maculatum*)	18 to 24 inches	Average to well-drained soil	Partial to full shade	3-8	✓			Red-brown leaves provide backdrop to small pink and lilac flowers in late spring. Seeds for birds.	Northeast
Indian Pink (*Spigelia marilandica*)	24 to 28 inches tall and 20 to 24 inches wide	Average to moist, well-drained soils	Full to part shade	5-9	✓			Crimson-red, trumpet-shaped flowers with yellow edges attract hummingbirds in spring.	Southeast, partial Southwest
Bronze Wave Coral Bells (*Heuchera villosa* 'Bronze Wave')	18 to 24 inches tall and wide	Prefers dry soil	Partial shade to full sun	3-8	✓	✓		Pink flowers rise above bronze-purple leaves in late spring and early summer. Blooms attract hummingbirds.	Northeast, Southeast, Midwest
Fringed Bleeding Heart (*Dicentra eximia*)	1 to 1.5 feet tall and wide	Rich, moist well-drained soil	Partial shade	3-9	✓			Small pink flowers resemble split open hearts beginning in spring and continue on and off throughout summer.	Northeast, partial Southeast
Red Bearberry (*Arctostaphylos uva-ursi*)	6 to 12 inches tall and 6 feet wide	Dry to moist spots	Full sun to shade	2-7	✓			White and pink flowers in spring followed by berries.	Northeast, Midwest, partial Southeast, partial West, partial Southwest
Red Columbine (*Aquilegia canadensis*)	3 to 4 feet tall and about 1 foot wide	Dry, well-drained soil	Partial to full shade	3-8	✓			Red and yellow flowers attract hummingbirds. Finches eat the seeds.	Northeast, Southeast, part Midwest
ZigZag Golden-rod (*Solidago flexicaulis*)	1 to 4 foot tall flower stems	Moist soil	Dappled shade	2-9	✓			Elongated yellow flower clusters mature into red fruit that are eaten by sparrows.	Midwest, Southeast, Northeast
Jack-in-the-Pulpit (*Arisaema triphyllum*)	Up to 2 feet tall	Moist to wet soil	Shade	4-9	✓			Easy to grow and produces berries that birds find attractive.	Northeast, Southeast, Midwest, some Southwest

Plant name	Plant size	Water needs	Preferred lighting conditions	Hardy to (USDA zones)	Provides 🌼 🌲🌲 🪺			Main season of interest	Native range
Purple Turtle-head (*Chelone obliqua*)	24 to 36 inches tall and 18 to 24 inches wide	Moist to wet soil	Full sun to dappled sun	5-9	✓			Flowers attract hummingbirds.	Southeast
Cinnamon Fern (*Osmunda cinnamomeum*)	Up to 6 feet tall	Moist to wet	Sun to shade	4-11			✓	The fuzz on the fiddleheads provide nesting material for birds.	Northeast, Southeast, Midwest
Virginia Creeper (*Parthenocissus quinquefolia*)	If allowed, will spread up to 40 feet	Moist	Sun to shade	5-11	✓	✓		Blue berries attract a variety of birds.	Northeast, Southeast, some Midwest
Golden Alex-ander (*Zizia aurea*)	Up to 3 feet tall	Medium moisture, well-drained soil	Sun to part shade	4-8	✓			Host plant for Black Swallowtail butterflies. Attractive to native insects.	Northeast, Southeast

A Red-eyed Vireo searches for insects to eat from its shady perch.

Jamie Weiss

Jamie Weiss has been sharing the importance of conservation practices throughout her career.

📍 NORTHERN COLORADO

One of the biggest bird conservation threats is habitat loss. Jamie Weiss has seen this firsthand in her previous role as the Habitat Hero Coordinator for Audubon Rockies, regional office of the National Audubon Society serving Colorado, Wyoming, and Utah.

The increased urbanization along Interstate 25 (I-25) has resulted in extreme population growth. I-25 is a north–south corridor that connects Colorado Springs and Denver—and also provides some of the highway's most scenic views of the Rocky Mountains and its foothills.

"As our communities grow, the native plants that birds, pollinators, and other wildlife depend on are vanishing. Creating living landscapes in our suburban/urban environments is essential," Jamie explained.

Habitat Heroes are people who practice a form of landscape stewardship, called **wildscaping**— landscaping designed to attract and benefit birds, pollinators, and other wildlife. The program is geared toward individuals who live in Colorado, Wyoming, and Utah. "The Habitat Hero program provides people, businesses, and cities with the resources to create bird habitat in their own communities."

"By planting bird-friendly gardens with native plants, not only are we creating more beautiful and water-efficient communities; we're connecting people to nature," she said. Because native plants have co-evolved with our harsh climate and surrounding ecosystems, by selecting plants that are adapted to your local climate, you'll minimize or eliminate the need for water, fertilizers, and pesticides, she explained.

The connection and "a-ha" moments help underscore the importance of preserving parcels of land to benefit the birds.

Prior to working at Audubon, Jamie worked for Colorado State Parks & Wildlife. To celebrate World Migratory Bird Day, various educational stations were set up at Boyd Lake State Park.

"I was running the 'bird migration' educational station, which comprised of an obstacle course to show the grueling tasks and obstacles birds may face during migration. One elementary-aged boy ran the obstacle course many times over because he enjoyed selecting the fate card at the end—showcasing that sometimes it just boils down to luck on survival," she said. "The fascination and excitement that one game brought to that child made me a believer that birds are a great way to connect with nature. (And that they are always around us!)"

Jamie also enjoys birding with her children. "I personally like to go birding with the family during the winter once the leaves have fallen, making identification a little easier and the trails are quieter too," she said. "Seeing bird conservation through the lens of little kids brings such joy. The basics of birding and flipping through guidebooks become less relied on, while observing birds takes the center stage which allows for connecting with nature more."

As concern for pollinators, water conservation, pesticide and fertilizer use grows, so does gardeners' interest in them. The Habitat Hero program can connect you to the large network of bird-friendly gardeners. "The Habitat Hero program offers a variety of ways to empower engagement through educational programs, robust volunteer network, certification process and connections to resources and partners," she said. "By creating bird-friendly gardens of our own we can help stitch back our fractured landscape one garden at a time and quite literally bring conservation home!"

A beautiful Habitat Hero project!

Water-wise native garden

A stately planter and a combination of native plants inside is perfect for adding along walkways and driveways, or even as a complement to the front entry. The sample plants included offer a variety of bloom throughout the growing season, and will attract other desirable species as well, such as monarch butterflies thanks to the inclusion of Butterfly Milkweed (*Asclepias tuberosa*) and Blazing Star (*Liatris scariosa*). The purple-flowering Agastache and pink-flowering coneflower begin blooming in mid-summer and continue into early fall, gradually transforming into the season of seeds as the flowers age and the finches stop to enjoy.

Additional varieties of coneflower can be included in this planting as well, such as Yellow Coneflower (*Echinacea paradoxa*) and Tennessee Coneflower (*Echinacea tennesseensis*). All *Echinacea* species pair beautifully with ornamental grasses such as Shenandoah Switch Grass (*Panicum virgatum* 'Shenandoah'). The planter chosen for this project has a self-watering insert, with the option for excess water to drain away. A large container with drainage holes will also work—look for one with the following size dimensions: 17½ inches high by 33 inches wide and with a 16 inch diameter.

A planter can be filled with a variety of water-wise native plants, including Agastache, echinacea, and native grasses.

BIRDS ATTRACTED

 Pigeons & Doves

 Finches

 Hummingbirds

 Blackbirds & Orioles

 New World Sparrows

Butterfly Milkweed (*Asclepias* spp.) is great for mid-season color.

Purple Coneflower (*Echinacea purpurea*) does beautifully in containers.

THIS WATER-WISE NATIVE GARDEN FEATURES THE FOLLOWING NATIVE PLANTS

Plant name	Plant size	Water needs	Preferred lighting conditions	Hardy to (USDA zones)	Provides 🌼	🌲🌲	🪺	Main season of interest	Native range
Butterfly Milkweed (*Asclepias tuberosa*)	1 to 3 feet tall	Dry to moist soil	Full sun	3-9	✓			Host plant for butterfly species such as the monarch. Hummingbirds will feed from orange flowers.	Northeast, Southeast, Midwest, partial Southwest
Purple Haze Anise Hyssop (*Agastache* 'Purple Haze')	Up to 3 feet tall	Good drainage	Full sun	4-8	✓			Purple/blue flowers in mid-late summer.	Midwest
Common Tarweed (*Madia elegans*)	2 feet tall	Well-drained soil, tolerant of dry conditions	Full sun	6-11	✓			Long-blooming annual, branching yellow daisy flowers on strong stems.	West
Yellow Coneflower (*Echinacea paradoxa*)	24 to 30 inches tall	Well-drained, lean soil. Drought-tolerant	Full sun	3-9	✓			Golden yellow flowers with dark purple cones, July through September.	Midwest
Blazing Star (*Liatris scariosa*)	2 to 4 feet tall	Medium, well-drained soil	Full sun	3-9	✓			Blooms mid-summer to early fall with spikes of purple tassel-like flowers.	Northeast, some Southeast
Shenandoah Switch Grass (*Panicum virgatum* 'Shenandoah')	3 to 4 feet tall and 18 to 24 inches wide	Dry to wet	Full sun to partial shade	4-9	✓	✓	✓	Red color in fall with small red flower plumes. Fall and winter interest. Hosts native caterpillars and provides food for birds.	Northeast, Southeast, Midwest, Southwest, partial West
Tennessee Coneflower (*Echinacea tennesseensis*)	2 to 2.5 feet tall and 1 to 2 feet wide	Lean, well-drained soil	Full sun to part shade	5-9	✓			Long, up-turned purple petals with coppery center cones. Flowers follow the sun throughout the day.	Only one state: Tennessee
Purple Coneflower (*Echinacea purpurea*)	2 to 4 feet tall and 2 feet wide	Dry, well-drained soil	Full sun to part shade	4-9	✓			Blooms early summer through fall, produces seeds for birds. Also attractive to butterflies and native bees.	Midwest, some Southeast, Northeast

Yellow Coneflower (*Echinacea paradoxa*) provides early season color.

Native plant container gardening

Many native plants can easily be adapted to grow in containers of various sizes. Container gardens work well in paved areas or spots with compacted soil that would be difficult to plant in. Window boxes, hanging planters, and whiskey barrels are great options for single or mixed species of plants. When choosing the appropriate pot or container, be sure to consider the soil and water preferences of the plant. Look for plants that share similar water and light requirements. Terra cotta pots allow the plant roots to breathe through the clay material. Other native plants that prefer moist soil will grow well in plastic or glazed ceramic containers.

Be sure the container has a drainage hole for excess water to escape—no drainage can cause roots to rot. Larger native plants, such as shrubs, should be planted in sizeable containers to prevent them from getting rootbound too quickly. (Rootbound means that there is a disproportionate area of roots to soil in the pot, leaving little or no space for further growth.) Choose a pot that is larger than the planting container the native plant was in coming home from the nursery. Place potted plants in an unheated garage, or wrap the base of the pot in burlap to help protect the roots in extreme cold temperatures.

A Carolina Wren closely examines aster (*Symphyotrichum* spp.) plants in late fall, looking for insects that may be hiding or overwintering on the stems.

BIRDS ATTRACTED

 Wood Warblers

 Cardinals, Grosbeaks & Buntings

 Crows, Magpies & Jays

 Nuthatches

 Woodpeckers

 Thrushes

 Wrens

 Vireos

 Waxwings

 New World Sparrows

 Chickadees & Titmice

 Mockingbirds & Thrashers

 Blackbirds & Orioles

Included on pages 92-93, are native plants that work well in small spaces—either individually or combined in a container.

SQUARE PLANTER

Use a square planter that measures a minimum of 16 × 16 × 16 inches. It can fit five small plants. The aster in this project is a western native, but asters that are native to your region can be substituted in.

HANGING BASKET

Hanging baskets can be used to house one or two small native plants. Consider the following minimum dimensions when choosing a hanging basket: 12 to 13 inches wide and at least 6 inches deep. Choose native plants that will do well in the available lighting in your designated space. The six plants on page 93, work well individually or grouped together.

A square container can be used for compact varieties of native plants, including coreopsis and gaillardia.

Hanging baskets can house a variety of native plants for tight spaces. In this container, a Virginia Strawberry (*Fragaria virginiana*) has enough space to develop healthy roots while allowing the runners to dangle downward. You can use the small "child" plants from the runners to start new plants in additional containers.

THIS NATIVE PLANT SQUARE CONTAINER FEATURES THE FOLLOWING NATIVE PLANTS

Plant name	Plant size	Water needs	Preferred lighting conditions	Hardy to (USDA zones)	Provides			Main season of interest	Native range
					✿	▲▲	☁		
Woodland Stonecrop (*Sedum ternatum*)	3 to 6 inches tall and 10 to 12 inches wide	Moist soil	Full sun to part sun	4-8	✔			Primarily a host plant for butterflies, this is the only sedum native to the U.S.	Northeast, Southeast and partial Midwest
Blanket Flower (*Gaillardia pulchella*)	1.5 to 2 feet tall	Sandy, well-draining soil	Full sun	2-11	✔			Highly drought-tolerant. Good pollinator plant that also attracts hummingbirds. Seedheads attract goldfinches.	Southeast
Pixie Fountain Tufted Hair Grass (*Deschampsia cespitosa* 'Pixie Fountain')	20 to 24 inches tall and 18 to 20 inches wide	Moist, well-drained soils	Full sun to part shade	2-7	✔			Late summer seeds provide food for birds.	West, Northeast, partial Southwest, partial Midwest
California Aster (*Symphyotrichum chilense* (formerly *Aster chilensis*))	1 to 3 feet tall	Loamy clay soil, drought-tolerant	Part shade to full sun	6-10	✔			Flowers bloom August through October, seeds afterwards provide food for birds. Host plant for caterpillars.	West
Lance-leaf Coreopsis (*Coreopsis lanceolata*)	2.5 feet tall	Sandy, gravely soil, loamy	Sun, part shade and shade	4-9	✔			Birds will eat seeds.	Northeast, Southeast, partial West, Midwest and Southwest

THE FOLLOWING NATIVE PLANTS WORK WELL IN HANGING BASKETS

Plant name	Plant size	Water needs	Preferred lighting conditions	Hardy to (USDA zones)	Provides 🌸 🌲🌲 🪺			Main season of interest	Native range
Virginia Strawberry (*Fragaria virginiana*)	6 inches	Dry to moist soil	Sun to shade	3-8	✓			Blooms April-June followed by fruits—works well as a groundcover.	Northeast, Southwest, West, Midwest
Pilgrim Cranberry (*Vaccinium macrocarpon* 'Pilgrim')	6 to 12 inches tall and 18 to 24 inches wide	Moist, well-drained soil	Sun to partial shade	4-8	✓			White to pink flowers in May followed by dark red tart fruit.	Northeast, Midwest
Lowbush Blueberry (*Vaccinium angustifolium*)	6 to 8 inches	Dry to moist soil	Full sun to shade	2-8	✓			Fruit appears in July through August.	Northeast, some Midwest
Little Goldstar Black-eyed Susan (*Rudbeckia fulgida* 'Little Goldstar')	14 to 16 inches tall and wide	Average, well-drained soil	Full sun to part shade	4-10	✓			Leave seedheads to feed birds in fall and winter.	Midwest
Appalachian Sedge (*Carex appalachica*)	6 inches tall and 15 to 18 inches wide	Well-drained, dry soil	Partial to full shade	3-7	✓			Wispy appearance. Flowers in spring attract pollinators and seeds will feed birds.	Northeast, partial Southeast
Dwarf Crested Iris (*Iris cristata*)	6 inches tall	Moist to dry soil	Part shade to shade	5-7	✓			Blue to white flowers in spring attract hummingbirds.	Southeast, some Midwest

📍 HAMDEN, CONNECTICUT

Fueling for an endurance event requires the right type of food to draw energy from. Jillian Bell learned this firsthand when she trained and ran the New York Marathon. It also helped her understand why certain native plants are more valuable as "fuel" for birds during their migration.

"There are specific nutritional needs to make the journey successful," she said. "It's similar to eating candy versus proteins and carb loading in preparation for a marathon. It really resonated with me."

Jillian uses this example when she visits schools to help children understand the importance of what birds need to successfully complete their migratory journeys. As a Program Associate for a bird-friendly community program in New York and Connecticut, Jillian shares how birds need to get to the prime nesting sites to have their pick of a mate and access to all the insects needed to rear their young.

She's also had the opportunity to work with and empower students to create schoolyard habitats and other bird-friendly habitats in open spaces. The schoolyard gardens also provide students with ownership of the space—from planting, caring for, and designing it. Even though each garden has the same intention—to use native plants and be bird-friendly—each garden is so unique. In one schoolyard garden the students wanted to have a rainbow garden, and had each color represented through the blooms on the native plants that they chose. At another school, Jillian helped create a sensory garden to provide a calm space. "It was making a difference for birds and the school community," she said.

Jillian Bell grows native plants, such as Butterfly Milkweed (*Asclepias tuberosa*), in her front garden.

It's not just gardens and plants that help Jillian share her knowledge with the community. When working with students, she will reference the pigeon to help kids learn about birds. "I love pigeons—they are so accessible," she said. "You can learn so much about birdwatching by 'practicing' on a pigeon, you can identify bird body parts, markings, etc. They were the birds I saw the most when I was growing up."

Looking into her front and back garden, Jillian assesses if the plants available are giving the energy amounts the birds need for their over-wintering, nesting, and migration—from the first arrival in spring and throughout each season. Jillian lives near East Rock Park in New Haven, Connecticut, which is a hotspot for birders in the spring because of the many migrants that move through the area.

One of the earliest plants to bloom in her garden is Red Columbine (*Aquilegia canadensis*), followed by the flowers of one of her favorite native plants, serviceberry (*Amelanchier* spp.) in the spring. "It's verdant green in the summer, and gets berries in the summer—it's literally bringing all the birds to the yard," she said, smiling. "It's also great for pollinators, and good for people who do not have a lot of space."

Jillian said she has always had a connection to plants since she was younger, and helps others in her community see the relationship between birds and native plants. "If I want a purple flower," she says, "why not plant the one that will bring the goldfinch?" (By the way, it's *Echinacea purpurea*).

Her front garden has helped initiate conversations with neighbors, and Jillian also uses the garden to explain how choosing native plants helps birds and pollinators. One neighbor keeps track of the monarch caterpillars that feed on the Butterfly Milkweed, and others will ask questions about plants and take photos to learn more. "We took the grass out of our 'hellstrip' and planted a lot of different things in there," she said. The variety of plants and birds increased greatly over two and a half years since she and her husband began modifying the property. In that time, she has relied less on bird feeders offering seed to attract birds to her garden, and let the plants do the work instead. "We planted our bird feeders," she said.

Jillian also incorporates native plants, such as asters, in her container gardens as well. "It's so fun to see the Black-capped Chickadee dangling upside down, holding on to the aster and trying to eat the tiny seeds."

This image of Jillian Bell and her hellstrip/median garden show how beautiful it can be to put birds front and center in your landscape.

Condo-friendly plantings

Many condo owners are required to follow the rules of a Home Owners Association (HOA), which aims to create a repetitive, consistent look throughout the grounds. Some guidelines make sense, such as not allowing invasive species into planting areas. There is usually a maintenance fee to provide upkeep to the common area plantings (and lawn areas).

One of the most important conversations may not be on the type of plants incorporated, but on the elimination of pesticides and herbicides that are used on the grounds as part of preventive maintenance.

Using native plants that meet design standards and criteria—instead of popularized non-native varieties such as Common Boxwood (*Buxus sempervirens*) and Japanese Holly (*Ilex crenata*)—will begin to pave the way to have productive conversations about incorporating plants that are eco-friendly and help the environment (and of course, our birds!). A reminder for HOA committees or board members is that native plants have adapted to the surrounding environment and will require less care in the long run than a plant considered non-native or exotic, which may appeal to budget concerns.

Guidelines may include focus plants that will look attractive throughout the seasons. Some HOA residents are allowed to include small shrubs, while others are limited to annuals and perennials. While some condo owners may not have the ability to plant in ground, they may be able to use native plants in pots and containers instead. Residents who live in HOA communities should find out if the community has a strict plant list that they encourage condo owners to abide by, or if there are general rules in places (such as, "annuals and perennials are okay to plant; no shrubs").

While the rules of HOAs can vary greatly, the following are a series of plants to consider for working within the parameters of HOA rules.

Even condos can provide habitat for birds.

BIRDS ATTRACTED

 Finches

Thrushes

 New World Sparrows

Hummingbirds

Generally, this list includes shrubs that are native (sometimes native cultivars for the compact size) and perennials that are container-friendly. Shamrock Inkberry (*Ilex glabra* 'Shamrock') stays more compact than the straight species. This shrub will maintain its leaves in the winter, and would work as a border edging or along a foundation planting, if allowed. The mounding variety of Oregon Boxwood (*Paxistima myrsinites*) will grow to 3 feet tall, and provides cover for birds.

The dwarf variety of Atlantic White Cedar, *Chamaecyparis thyoides* 'Top Point', is a slow-growing evergreen that keeps a columnar shape, making it a tidy option for foundation gardens. It can be spaced 16 to 20 inches apart at planting and will gradually grow to create a full hedge that will provide cover for birds. It can also work well individually in containers on a small condo patio area, but will need to be watered a bit more regularly. The foliage is bluish-green during the growing season and then changes to plum and bronze coloring in colder weather. The tiny berries that are produced in the fall (along with being a larval host plant for butterflies) also feed birds. It is drought-tolerant once established.

Slightly more free form, but still compact in size, is Gemo Dense Kalm's St. John's Wort (*Hypericum kalmiannum* 'Gemo'). It is deciduous, meaning it will drop its leaves in winter, but offers bright yellow flowers that are attractive to bees and hummingbirds. It provides cover for birds in the summer and birds, such as finches, will eat the seed in the winter months.

Pairing Woodland Stonecrop (*Sedum ternatum*) and Dwarf Crested Iris (*Iris cristata*) together will make a nice low perennial border that will help suppress weeds. Also consider including dwarf varieties of *Rudbeckia* spp. in containers to provide summer color.

A Carolina Wren perches on a garden statue. Eliminating the use of pesticides plays an important role in keeping small birds like this healthy.

CONDO-FRIENDLY NATIVE PLANTS THAT WILL STAY FAIRLY COMPACT

Plant name	Plant size	Water needs	Preferred lighting conditions	Hardy to (USDA zones)	Provides ✿	🌲	🪺	Main season of interest	Native range
Top Point Atlantic White Cedar (*Chamaecyparis thyoides* 'Top Point')	4 to 5 feet tall and 2 to 3 feet wide	Average, well-drained soil	Full sun	4-8		✓		Berries in fall. Winter color in landscape.	Northeast, Southeast
Gemo Dense Kalm's St. John's Wort (*Hypericum kalmiannum* 'Gemo')	2 to 3 feet tall and wide	Average to dry, well-drained soil	Full sun to partial shade	4-9	✓	✓		Provides cover for birds in summer. Finches eat seeds. Hummingbirds attracted to flowers. Drought-tolerant once established.	Midwest
Bar Harbor Creeping Juniper (*Juniperus horizontalis* 'Bar Harbor')	1 foot tall and spreads 6 to 8 feet wide	Average to dry soil, likes sandy soil	Sun to part sun	3-9		✓		Provides cover for wildlife—works well with foundations, slopes, walls, and walkways.	Northeast
Little Goldstar Black-eyed Susan (*Rudbeckia fulgida* 'Little Goldstar')	14 to 16 inches tall and wide	Average, well-drained soil	Full sun to part shade	4-10	✓			Leave seedheads to feed birds in fall and winter.	Midwest
Woodland Stonecrop (*Sedum ternatum*)	3 to 6 inches tall and 10 to 12 inches wide	Moist soil	Full sun to part sun	4-8	✓			Primarily a host plant for butterflies, this is the only native sedum in the U.S.	Northeast, Southeast and partial Midwest
Dwarf Crested Iris (*Iris cristata*)	6 inches tall	Moist to dry soil	Part shade to shade	5-7	✓			Blue to white flowers in spring attract hummingbirds.	Southeast, some Midwest
Shamrock Inkberry (*Ilex glabra* 'Shamrock')	4 feet tall and wide	Adaptable to all soils	Full sun	4-11	✓	✓		Songbirds eat berries produced in the fall. This variety is more compact than the straight species of *Ilex glabra*.	Eastern coast
Oregon Boxwood (*Paxistima myrsinites*)	1 to 3 feet tall and 2 to 4 feet wide	Moist to dry, well-drained soil	Partial shade	3-9		✓		Mounding species will provide cover for small birds.	West

Black-eyed Susans (*Rudbeckia* spp.) are available in smaller cultivar varieties, which can be used either in low foundation plantings or containers.

Shamrock Inkberry (*Ilex glabra* 'Shamrock') is a smaller variety that fits well in compact spaces. You will need both a male and female plant for pollination to ensure berries.

Gemo Dense Kalm's St John's Wort (*Hypericum kalmiannum* 'Gemo') flowers are attractive to hummingbirds and bees.

West coast window box

The red tubular blooms of Marian Sampson Hummingbird Coyote Mint (*Monardella macrantha* 'Marian Sampson') attract hummingbirds.

When planning a container planting to attract hummingbirds, many of the popular flowers to include happen to be red. Part of the appeal of this color is due to a hummingbird's eyes being more "tuned in" to red and yellow colors, due to the dense concentration of cones in the retina. Colors such as blue are more muted for hummingbirds. This isn't to say that they will not visit other color flowers, because nectar in a flower is important as well. Tubular-shaped flowers are also attractive to hummingbirds, making it easier for them to feed from the flowers with their long bills.

Anna's Hummingbirds and Allen's Hummingbirds will visit feeders and flowering plants and are primarily found along the west coast of the United States year-round. This window box project focuses primarily on west coast plants, but when assembling a window box planting for other regions, include colorful natives to lure hummingbirds in. You can also pair your window box garden with a hummingbird feeder to provide additional food.

The plants featured on the next page allow you to offer blooms to visiting hummingbirds without having access to a large amount of land (similar to the Native Plant Container Garden on page 90).

Firecracker bush close-up in window box.

Hummingbirds will be drawn to native flowers.

Hummer facts

Did you know? Hummingbirds are one of the few animals that can hover, which means remaining in one place in the air without moving forwards or backwards, up or down. This is because their wings are shaped for this purpose with strong muscles. They flap their wings faster than any other bird—more than 4,000 wingbeats per minute!

BIRDS ATTRACTED

 Hummingbirds   Finches

NATIVE PLANTS TO INCORPORATE INTO WINDOW BOX DESIGNS

Plant name	Plant size	Water needs	Preferred lighting conditions	Hardy to (USDA zones)	Provides ✿ 🌲🌲 🪺			Main season of interest	Native range
Firecracker Bush (*Bouvardia ternifolia*)	Up to 3 to 4 feet tall and wide*	Fertile, well-drained soil	Full to part sun	9-11	✓			Hummingbirds are attracted to the red flowers.	Partial Southwest (and Central America)
Margarita BOP Penstemon (*Penstemon heterophyllus* 'Margarita BOP')	24 inches tall and wide	Fertile, well-drained soil	Sun to part sun	7-10	✓			Hummingbirds are attracted to the tubular shaped flowers in spring and summer.	West
Butterfly Milkweed (*Asclepias tuberosa*)	1 to 3 feet tall	Dry to moist soil	Full sun	3-9	✓			Host plant for butterfly species. Hummingbirds feed from orange flowers.	Northeast, Southeast, Midwest, partial Southwest
Wild Canterbury Bells (*Phacelia minor*)	Up to 2 feet	Little water	Full sun	4-10	✓			Annual herb that produces blue to purple bell-shaped flowers.	West
California Poppy (*Eschscholzia californica*)	1 to 2 feet tall	Well-draining, drought-tolerant	Full sun	3-9	✓			Flowers March through May but extended bloom with added water.	West
Desert Verbena (*Glandularia gooddingii*)	6 to 12 inches tall	Coarse, well-draining soil	Full sun	4-7	✓			Hummingbirds feed from purple flowers that bloom spring through fall. Finches eat the seeds.	West
Desert Zinnia (*Zinnia acerosa*)	6 to 10 inches tall and up to 2 feet wide	Sandy, coarse, well-draining soil	Full sun	6-9	✓			Low-mounding plant with white flowers attracts pollinators and hummingbirds.	West
San Diego Sage (*Salvia munzii*)	1.5 to 3 feet tall and 3 feet wide	Well-drained soil	Full sun	9-11	✓			Compact with purple flowers that are attractive to hummingbirds.	West
Mojave Kingcup Cactus (*Echinocereus mojavensis*)	9 inches tall by 5 inches wide	Sandy, well-draining soil	Full sun to part shade	6-10	✓			Red flowers attract hummingbirds. Birds will eat fruit.	West
Desert Sand-Verbena (*Abronia villosa*)	3 to 6 inches tall and 1 to 2 feet wide	Sandy, fast-draining soil	Full sun	8-10	✓			Purple flowers attract hummingbirds. Flowers are scented at night which attracts moths.	West

When grown in a window box as an annual it will not grow to full size.

Moisture-rich garden

Not all gardens have the ideal soil conditions, but thankfully the diversity of native plants in North America provides variety for home gardeners. Garden areas with heavy clay soil that retains water can be a challenge for many of the sun-loving plants that thrive in dry soils. There are many native plants that thrive in the opposite soil conditions.

The term "moisture-rich" gardens can encompass a variety of environments, such as wet prairies, edges of ponds and rivers, ditches, and brackish or freshwater swamps. It can also include garden spots that are slow to dry out. The plants outlined are selections that will do well in sun to part shade. As with other garden plans, take stock of the amount of sunlight the garden receives in the spring, summer, and fall.

Spicebush (*Lindera benzoin*) will produce red berries in the late summer and fall when a female and male plant are present in the garden. The berries are usually devoured quickly by migrating and resident birds, such as this female Northern Cardinal.

BIRDS ATTRACTED

 Cardinals, Grosbeaks & Buntings

 Woodpeckers

 Thrushes

 Finches

 Wood Warblers

 Mockingbirds & Thrashers

 Vireos

 Hummingbirds

There are many shrubs to choose from. Many of the early blooming willow (*Salix* spp.) varieties are not only one of the earliest blooming plants for native pollinators, but also feed a variety of birds as well. White-crowned Sparrows will eat the buds (or catkins) and the Yellow Warbler, Warbling Vireo, Philadelphia Vireo, and Common Grackle use willows as nesting sites (Illinois Wildflowers).

In spring, hummingbirds will be drawn to the flowers of Pinxterbloom Azalea (*Rhododendron periclymenoides*). This plant will sucker and spread slowly over time, so it is good for medium to large gardens. Another popular native is the Gray Dogwood (*Cornus racemosa*), which produces fruit that attracts Northern Cardinals, Downy Woodpeckers, Northern Flickers, and Eastern Bluebirds. It's also a host plant for the Spring Azure butterfly and the flowers attract many native pollinators in the spring.

Spicebush (*Lindera benzoin*) will also flower early in the spring, and has been commonly called the "forsythia of the woods" thanks to the muted yellow flowers that create a haze of yellow in the early spring when the woods are often bare. These flowers on the female plants will go on to produce red berries, which are devoured by birds during the fall migration.

Another native shrub known for the red berry display in the winter is Winterberry (*Ilex verticillata*). Also a dioecious species (needing a male and female plant), the red berries will remain on the branches after the leaves have dropped in late fall. The berries will attract American Robins, Hermit Thrushes, Eastern Bluebirds, Yellow-bellied Sapsuckers, and White-throated Sparrows.

For perennials, there's a variety of colorful flowers that will also do well in the moisture-rich garden. Sneezeweed (*Helenium autumnale*) is one of the plants that is native to the entire continental U.S.! Pruning in spring can keep the plant more compact—otherwise it can grow up to 5 feet tall and may need staking.

An Eastern Bluebird perches on a maple tree branch.

Sneezeweed will attract American Goldfinches once the flower heads turn to seed.

Great Blue Lobelia (*Lobelia siphilitica*) grows to 2 to 3 feet.

Joe Pye Weed (*Eutrochium maculatum*) is a host plant for several caterpillars. It also provides cover for birds in the garden due to its height.

Cardinal Flower (*Lobelia cardinalis*) features striking red flowers that depend on hummingbirds for pollination. It can be a short-lived perennial but will self-seed in a spot it is happy in.

Another *Lobelia* species that is also attractive to hummingbirds is the Great Blue Lobelia (*Lobelia siphilitica*). This plant also performs well in moist soil. Blooming throughout the summer, it adds the coveted color blue to the garden palette—a color that is sometimes hard to come by in flowers.

Swamp Milkweed (*Asclepias incarnata*) will be less aggressive than the common milkweed species, and also does well in wetter soils. It is also one of the milkweeds that supports the monarch butterfly.

The Swamp Mallow (*Hibiscus moscheutos*), also called Rose Mallow, adores wet soil. Each flower only blooms for a day, but the show begins in summer and extends through early autumn. The large, bright flowers attract hummingbirds, and it's also a host plant for several butterflies and moths. Birds also use the stem fibers for nesting material, while Red-winged Blackbirds may use swamp mallow as a nesting site. The seed also feeds other birds in winter.

Easy-to-grow Joe Pye Weed (*Eutrochium maculatum*) is a tall perennial plant that provides late summer color into early fall. The statuesque plants can be placed toward the back of the garden, and not only will the flowers attract hummingbirds, it is also an important stopover plant for the migrating monarch butterflies. If the straight species of Joe Pye Weed is too tall for your spot, consider some of the cultivar versions, such as 'Little Joe', for inclusion in the garden.

A Ruby-throated Hummingbird approaches the red bloom of a Cardinal Flower (*Lobelia cardinalis*).

THIS MOISTURE-RICH GARDEN FEATURES THE FOLLOWING NATIVE PLANTS

Plant name	Plant size	Water needs	Preferred lighting conditions	Hardy to (USDA zones)	Provides ❀	🌲🌲	🥧	Main season of interest	Native range
Common Sneezeweed (*Helenium autumnale*)	3 to 5 feet tall and 3 feet wide	Wet to moist soil	Sun to part sun	3-9	✔			Flowers begin in late summer and continue into fall.	All
Swamp (Rose) Mallow (*Hibiscus moscheutos*)	4 to 7 feet tall and 3 to 4 feet wide	Rich wet to moist soil	Full to part sun	5-8	✔		✔	Summer—with flowers attracting hummingbirds.	Northeast, Southeast, South
Swamp Milkweed (*Asclepias incarnata*)	Up to 5 feet tall and 2 to 3 feet wide	Moist to wet soil	Full sun	3-6	✔			The pink flowers are attractive to hummingbirds. The flowers also attract tiny insects that feed baby quail.	Northeast, Southeast
Joe Pye Weed (*Eutrochium maculatum,* formerly *Eupatorium purpureum*)	Up to 7 feet tall (although there are several shorter cultivars) 2 to 3 feet wide	Moist soil	Full sun	3-8	✔	✔		Flowers are attractive to hummingbirds and finches will eat the seeds. Host plant for 40+ butterfly and moth larvae.	Northeast, Southeast and Midwest
Swamp Sunflower (*Helianthus angustifolius*)	3 to 10 feet tall and 2 to 4 feet wide	Moist to wet soil	Sun	5-9	✔			Maturing seedheads will feed birds. Plants will spread so start with one.	Southeast, partial Northeast and partial Southwest
Cardinal Flower (*Lobelia cardinalis*)	1 to 6 feet tall	Moist soil	Sun to part shade	2-8	✔			Flowers are specialized for feeding hummingbirds.	Northeast, Southwest, Midwest and some Southwest
Buttonbush (*Cephalanthus occidentalis*)	6 to 12 feet or taller	Wet soil	Part shade to shade	5-9	✔			Seeds are attractive to ducks and shorebirds. Very popular with insects for nectar. Hummingbirds will also feed on flowers.	Northeast, Southeast, some Southwest

Plant name	Plant size	Water needs	Preferred lighting conditions	Hardy to (USDA zones)	Provides 🌸	🌲🌲	🪹	Main season of interest	Native range
Winterberry (*Ilex verticillata*)	6 to 15 feet tall	Dry to wet soil	Full sun to shade	3-9	✓			Red berries over winter. ***Need at least one male plant to pollinate female plants.**	Southeast, Northeast
White Turtlehead (*Chelone glabra*)	24 to 36 inches tall and 18 to 24 inches wide	Moist to wet soil	Part sun	3-8	✓		✓	Provides nesting material for birds. Flowers attract hummingbirds.	Southeast, Northeast, partial Midwest
Gray Dogwood (*Cornus racemosa*)	6 to 16 feet tall	Prefers moist soil but will adapt to drier sites	Full sun, part sun, part shade	4-8	✓		✓	White fruit appears in fall against red stems. Good source for caterpillars.	Northeast, Southeast, Midwest
Pinxterbloom Azalea (*Rhododendron periclymenoides*)	6 to 10 feet tall and 4 to 6 feet wide	Moist, well-drained and acidic soil	Part shade to part sun	4-9	✓			Large clusters of tubular flowers in white, pink, or purple will attract hummingbirds.	Southeast, Northeast
Spicebush (*Lindera benzoin*)	4 to 12 feet high and wide	Wet to well-drained, but can tolerate dry	Part shade to part sun	4-9	✓	✓		A female and male plant is needed to produce berries.	Northeast, Southeast, some West
Great Blue Lobelia (*Lobelia siphilitica*)	1 to 4 feet tall. Spreads 1 to 2 feet	Moist soil	Part to full shade	4-8	✓			Deep blue flower spikes are attractive to hummingbirds.	Northeast, Southeast, Midwest, some Southwest
Missouri River Willow (*Salix eriocephala*)	12 to 20 feet tall	Moist, sandy soil	Full to part sun	4-8	✓	✓		Provides food and nesting sites for birds. Plants are dioecious, so a male and female are needed to produce seeds.	Northeast, Southeast, some Midwest
Heart-leaved Willow (*Salix rigida*)	3 to 13 feet tall	Wet, loamy soil	Full to part shade	4-8	✓	✓		Provides food and nesting sites for birds. Plants are dioecious, so a male and female are needed to produce seeds.	Northeast, Midwest

Insect garden

Instead of trying to eliminate insects from the garden, put out the welcome mat for them. Small insects that seek out native plants for food, such as caterpillars, flies, and small wasps, will also attract insectivorous birds to the garden, such as Blue-gray Gnatcatchers and Eastern Phoebes. You may even get lucky and have a migrating bird stop by to hunt insects (beetles, gnats, and aphids), such as the Golden-crowned Kinglet and Ruby-crowned Kinglet. A good number of plants that attract insects also produce berries or seeds that birds will also eat.

River Oats/Sea Oats (*Chasmanthium latifolium*) is an ornamental grass that does well in a part sun to part shade area. It is also a host plant for several skipper butterflies, and the seeds will feed birds in late autumn to winter. This plant can self-seed, so keep an eye on small shoots if you want to contain it in one area. Combine River Oats with the pollinator plant Short Toothed Mountain Mint (*Pycnanthemum muticum*), Red Bee Balm (*Monarda didyma*), coneflower (*Echinacea* spp.) and Tufted Hairgrass (*Deschampsia cespitosa*) for a colorful plant design that will also attract hummingbirds and seed-eating birds, especially finches. The Tufted Hairgrass, along with the River Oats, will add movement to the garden on breezy days.

Pairing the bright colors of *Rudbeckia triloba* with the small white flowers of Slender Mountain Mint (*Pycnanthemum tenuifolium*) and White Goldenrod (*Solidago bicolor*) is also a powerful combination. Add a native sunflower, *Helianthus* species, to entice insects to the blooms and birds to the seeds. Asters (*Symphyotrichum* spp.) and goldenrod (*Solidago* spp.) also attract many native insects. Many birds—such as towhees, Indigo Buntings, and sparrows—will eat the aster seeds. Finches, juncos, chickadees, nuthatches, and titmice will return in late fall to eat the goldenrod seeds. Both pair well with the foliage colors of Little Bluestem (*Schizachyrium scoparium*). The seeds of Little Bluestem are eaten by Rosy Finches, Chipping Sparrows, Field Sparrows, and Tree Sparrows.

Blue Wood Aster (*Symphyotrichum cordifolium*), Joe Pye Weed (*Eutrochium maculatum*) seedheads, and yellow Goldenrod (*Solidago* spp.) blooms entice insects to visit the garden.

Heliopsis species are attractive to insects and recent cultivars offer a pop of color to the garden.

One of the best trees to include in an insect-themed garden is an oak tree, and the Dwarf Chestnut Oak Tree (*Quercus prinoides*) is one variety that will stay fairly compact. It will begin producing acorns when it is between three and five years old, which will attract jays, nuthatches, grackles, thrashers, titmice, towhees, and woodpeckers. As the plant matures, it will produce suckers, creating a thicket that provides further nesting habitat for songbirds.

Allegheny Serviceberry (*Amelanchier laevis*) is one of the earliest blooming native trees, and also an important food source for pollinators. After this tree blooms, it produces red fruit that is attractive to American Goldfinches, Tufted Titmice, Brown Thrashers, Blue Jays, Carolina Chickadees, Northern Cardinals, and American Robins. The Saskatoon Serviceberry (*Amelanchier alnifolia*) produces purple fruit that is attractive to Downy and Hairy Woodpeckers, Western Kingbirds, and Western Bluebirds. It can be paired with White Fringe Tree (*Chionanthus virginicus*), another small tree that is also tolerant of wind and air pollution. White fringe

tree will produce blue berries later in the season that are attractive to Blue Jays, Northern Cardinals, mockingbirds, and even wild turkeys. Interplant with Snowberry (*Symphoricarpos albus*), which will retain its white berries into the winter, feeding thrashers, Cedar Waxwings, Pine Grosbeaks, and American Robins.

Witch Hazel (*Hamamelis virginiana*) produces fragrant flowers in autumn with petals that resemble (often yellow) crumbled strips of paper. Spring Witch Hazel (*Hamamelis vernalis*) flowers in mid-winter. Both flower at times when nectar sources are scarce for native insects. The seeds from the plants are attractive to birds and full-grown shrubs provide nesting spots.

For gardeners located in southwestern Oregon and into California, consider adding Red Larkspur (*Delphinium nudicaule*) to the garden bed. This deciduous perennial is a host plant for moths, and the flowers are pollinated mainly by hummingbirds. The seeds can be eaten by finches.

American Goldfinches will eat the seeds of *Rudbeckia triloba*.

The flowers of White Fringe Tree (*Chionanthus virginicus*) are attractive to pollinators.

BIRDS ATTRACTED

 Thrushes

 Hummingbirds

 Finches

 Chickadees & Titmice

 Cardinals, Grosbeaks & Buntings

 Mockingbirds & Thrashers

 Blackbirds & Orioles

 Nuthatches

 Wrens

 New World Sparrows

 Woodpeckers

 Vireos

 Waxwings

 Crows, Magpies & Jays

 Wood Warblers

 Creepers

 Gnatcatchers

 Kinglets

Autumn Gold Willowleaf Sunflower (*Helianthus salicifolius* 'Autumn Gold') and Short Toothed Mountain Mint (*Pycnanthemum muticum*) are both attractive to a variety of native insects.

A Red-bellied Woodpecker climbs a Black Walnut tree. Black Walnut trees can be a great source of insect food, but the juglone in their roots is not compatible with many other plants growing nearby. If you have a Black Walnut tree in your garden, look for plant varieties that are juglone tolerant.

NATIVE PLANTS TO ATTRACT MORE NATIVE INSECTS

Plant name	Plant size	Water needs	Preferred lighting conditions	Hardy to (USDA zones)	Provides			Main season of interest	Native range
					🌸	🌲	🪹		
Short Toothed Mountain Mint (*Pycnanthemum muticum*)	24 to 26 inches tall and wide	Moist soil	Full sun to part shade	4-8	✓	✓		Attracts and feeds many insects, which in turn provides food for birds.	Northeast
Witch Hazel (*Hamamelis virginiana*)	15 to 20 feet tall and wide	Average soil moisture	Sun to part shade	3-8	✓		✓	Flowers in late fall. Birds eat the seeds after it falls to the ground. Upright branches are ideal nesting sites.	Northeast, Southeast
Pennsylvania Sedge (*Carex pensylvanica*)	8 to 10 inches tall and 12 to 18 inches wide	Well-drained to dry soil	Sun to shade	3-6	✓	✓		Larval host plant for insects. Seeds attract birds.	Northeast, Midwest
Snowberry (*Symphoricarpos albus*)	2 to 5 feet tall and 4 to 6 feet wide	Dry to moist soil	Full sun to shade	2-5	✓	✓	✓	Larval host plant. Berries in winter. **Note: fruit not edible for humans.**	Northeast, Midwest
Snowberry (*Symphoricarpos albus* var. *laevigatus*)	4 to 6 feet tall and 8 to 12 feet wide	Dry to moist soil	Shade	2-7	✓	✓		Hummingbirds like flowers. Berries attract thrushes. Larval host plant for native insects. **Note: fruit not edible for humans.**	Western
Slender Mountain Mint (*Pycnanthemum tenuifolium*)	2 to 3 feet tall	Moist, well-drained to dry soil	Sun, part shade	4-8	✓			Attracts many insects, which attracts birds.	Northeast, Southeast, partial Midwest, partial Southwest
New England Aster (*Symphyotrichum novae-angliae*)	2 to 6 feet tall	Moist soil	Partial shade	4-8	✓			Hummingbirds visit flowers. Songbirds eat the seeds.	Northeast
Calico Aster (*Symphyotrichum lateriflorum*)	2 to 3 feet tall and up to 3 feet wide	Average to dry soil	Full sun, partial sun, shade	3-9	✓			Larval host plant. Birds eat seeds.	Northeast, Midwest

Continued on next page

Plant name	Plant size	Water needs	Preferred lighting conditions	Hardy to (USDA zones)	Provides			Main season of interest	Native range
					✿	🌲	🪺		
Gemo Dense Kalm's St. John's Wort (*Hypericum kalmiannum* 'Gemo')	2 to 3 feet tall and wide	Average to dry, well-drained soil	Full sun to partial shade	4-9	✓	✓		Provides cover for birds in summer. Finches eat seeds. Hummingbirds attracted to the flowers. Drought-tolerant once established	Midwest
Allegheny Serviceberry (*Amelanchier laevis*)	15 to 25 feet tall and wide	Medium moist well-drained soil	Part sun/ shade	4-8	✓			Birds will eat the purple-black fruit in late summer. Leaves provide red autumn color.	Northeast, partial Midwest
Saskatoon Serviceberry (*Amelanchier alnifolia*)	4 to 18 feet tall	Dry, rocky soil	Full sun	4-8	✓			Small purple fruits will feed birds.	West, partial Midwest
White Fringe Tree (*Chionanthus virginicus*)	12 to 20 feet tall	Moist, well-drained soil	Full sun to part shade	4-9	✓			Fragrant white flowers in spring. Bluish fruit in early fall. A male and female plant is needed to set fruit.	Southeast
River Oats/Sea Oats (*Chasmanthium latifolium*)	2 to 3 feet tall and 1 to 2 feet wide	Moist soil	Part sun to part shade	5-8	✓		✓	Birds eat the seedheads and use the leaves for nesting materials. Can self-sow, but can be removed easily when young. Provides winter interest.	Southeast, partial Southwest, partial Northeast
Little Goldstar Black-eyed Susan (*Rudbeckia fulgida* 'Little Goldstar')	14 to 16 inches tall and wide	Average, well-drained soil	Full sun to part shade	4-10	✓			Leave seedheads to feed birds in fall and winter.	Midwest
Mellow Yellows Coneflower (*Echinacea purpurea* 'Mellow Yellows')	24 to 30 inches tall and 12 to 24 inches wide	Dry, well-drained soil	Full sun to part shade	4-9	✓			Provides nectar for pollinators and seedheads feed birds in fall.	Midwest, Southeast
Prairie Glow Black-eyed Susan (*Rudbeckia triloba* 'Prairie Glow')	3 to 4 feet tall and 1 to 2 feet wide	Average to moist soil	Full sun	4-8	✓			Flowers are attractive to native bees and butterflies. Seedheads feed birds in fall and winter. Will spread in ideal conditions.	Northeast, Midwest

Plant name	Plant size	Water needs	Preferred lighting conditions	Hardy to (USDA zones)	Provides			Main season of interest	Native range
					🌸	🌲	🪹		
White Goldenrod (*Solidago bicolor*)	2 to 3 feet tall and 1 to 2 feet wide	Dry to heavy clay soil	Sun to part shade	5-10	✔			Blooms in late summer and early fall which attracts native bees. Host plant for caterpillars and birds also eat the seeds.	Northeast
Dwarf Chestnut Oak Tree (*Quercus prinoides*)	12 to 20 feet tall and wide	Various soil with good drainage	Full sun	4-8	✔	✔	✔	Attracts several insect species for birds to eat. Produces acorns at an early age. Will provide cover and nesting areas for birds as it matures.	Northeast
Blue Wood Aster (*Symphyotrichum cordifolium*)	2 to 5 feet and 1.5 to 2 feet wide	Dry to moist soil	Full sun to part shade	3-8	✔			Attracts a wide variety of insects that birds will eat. Seeds provide food in late fall and winter.	Northeast, Midwest
Autumn Gold Willowleaf Sunflower (*Helianthus salicifolius* 'Autumn Gold')	24 to 48 inches tall and wide	Average, medium to well-drained soil	Full sun	5-9	✔			Birds are attracted to seedheads in fall.	Midwest
Tufted Hairgrass (*Deschampsia cespitosa*)	1 to 3 feet tall	Medium to moist soil	Partial sun	4-8	✔			Larval food plant for several butterflies. Late season color and provides winter interest in the garden.	Northeast, partial Midwest, West, partial Southwest, partial Southeast
Joe Pye Weed (*Eutrochium maculatum*, formerly *Eupatorium purpureum*)	Up to 7 feet tall (there are shorter cultivars) and 2 to 3 feet wide	Moist soil	Full sun	3-8	✔	✔		Flowers are attractive to hummingbirds and finches will eat the seeds. Host plant for 40+ butterfly and moth larvae.	Northeast, Southeast, Midwest
Red Bee Balm (*Monarda didyma*)	24 to 48 inches tall	Well-drained soil	Full sun to part sun	4-9	✔			Scarlet red flowers attract hummingbirds.	Northeast, some Midwest, some Southeast
Little Bluestem (*Schizachyrium scoparium*)	18 to 24 inches tall and 12 inches wide	Low	Sun to part shade	3-9	✔	✔	✔	Color changes from blue green to red in fall into winter. Will spread in larger landscapes. Seeds feed birds.	Northeast, Midwest, West, Southwest, Southeast
Red Larkspur/ Canyon Delphinium (*Delphinium nudicaule*)	1 to 2 feet tall and wide	Well-drained, moist to dry soil	Part shade to shade	7-9	✔			Red flowers in spring are attractive to hummingbirds. Also provides food for birds as a host plant and with seeds.	West

Sunny hummingbird and songbird garden

It's not surprising that there are many plants to choose from when creating a garden that satisfies the desires of both hummingbirds and songbirds. The flowers also attract several pollinators and other native insects that will also be food for songbirds and hummingbirds. As the flowers age and turn to seed, they will feed songbirds into the colder months.

Flowering plants look great in groups of three, clustered together to produce a swath of color, but including one of each species will also create a colorful tapestry that blooms throughout the seasons. The recommended shrubs and small trees can be added as singular specimens to highlight the flowering plants. These plants can be included in larger garden spaces by increasing the number of each species of plants included.

Most commonly the flowers that tend to attract hummingbirds are red tubular-shaped flowers, but they will visit orange, red-yellow, pink, and other colors of flowers as well. At least 20 species of native plants in the northeast are pollinated primarily by hummingbirds.

A selection of native plants that peak in bloom in autumn.

The number is even higher in the western U.S. with 130 plant species pollinated by hummingbirds. The attractive plants also usually do not have a scent and lack a spot to rest and perch (Johnsgard 1997).

Bush Honeysuckle (*Diervilla lonicera*) has small yellow flowers that attract hummingbirds. It is a medium-size shrub that is also tolerant of urban pollution, making it a good candidate to include in an inner-city environment. (It does share the same common name—bush honeysuckle—as the invasive *Lonicera japonica*, so make sure you add the correct variety to your garden space.)

Redbuds (either *Cercis canadensis* or *Cercis occidentalis*, depending on your location) are great trees to include in a bird-friendly garden. They attract Chickadees & Titmice, as well as warblers, woodpeckers, vireos, and flycatchers, who use the tree as a food source for the insects it attracts and the seedpods it produces.

Coneflowers (*Echinacea* spp.), bee balms (*Monarda* spp.) and Common Sneezeweed (*Helenium autumnale*) offer a colorful combination that can be planted beneath redbuds or Chokeberries (*Aronia melanocarpa*).

Both Compass Plants (*Silphium laciniatum*) and Cup Plant (*Silphium perfoliatum*) offer yellow flowers that attract hummingbirds and later produce seeds that attract American Goldfinches. While both grow fairly large and can be placed toward the back of the plant border, the Cup Plant also has the ability to hold water within the leaves, which also attracts birds and other small animals looking for a drink.

Eastern Redbuds (*Cercis canadensis*) attract insectivorous birds in early spring due to the insects that use it as a host plant. The nectar in the pink flowers also attracts hummingbirds. Some varieties produce white flowers instead of pink.

Black-eyed Susan (*Rudbeckia fulgida*) is a Midwest native plant that blooms late summer into fall. Leave the perennial flower stems standing into the winter months to provide seed for birds.

The flowers of Common Sneezeweed (*Helenium autumnale*) are attractive to several native insects.

The brilliant red flowers of Red Bee Balm (*Monarda didyma*) will draw the hummingbirds to the garden.

The petite blossoms of native Bush Honeysuckle (*Diervilla lonicera*) are attractive to hummingbirds.

Spotted Bee Balm (*Monarda punctata*) offers flowers that are attractive to hummingbirds.

The blooms of Black-eyed Susan (*Rudbeckia fulgida*) and Purple Coneflower (*Echinacea purpurea*) intermingle with the seedheads of Anise Hyssop (*Agastache foeniculum*), Goldenrod (*Solidago* spp.) and Mistflower (*Conoclinium coelestinum*).

BIRDS ATTRACTED

 Hummingbirds

 Finches

 Chickadees & Titmice

 Thrushes

 Waxwings

 Mockingbirds & Thrashers

 Woodpeckers

 Vireos

THIS SUNNY HUMMINGBIRD AND SONGBIRD GARDEN FEATURES THE FOLLOWING NATIVE PLANTS

Plant name	Plant size	Water needs	Preferred lighting conditions	Hardy to (USDA zones)	Provides			Main season of interest	Native range
Bush Honeysuckle (*Diervilla lonicera*)	2 to 3 feet tall and 2 to 5 feet wide	Dry to moist soil	Full sun to part shade	3-7	✔	✔	✔	Yellow flowers attract hummingbirds. Dry fruit feeds songbirds in the fall. Colorful foliage in landscape. Two or more shrubs are recommended.	Northeast, partial Midwest, partial Southeast
Chokeberry (*Aronia melanocarpa*)	5 to 6 feet tall and wide	Moist, well-draining soil	Full sun	3-8	✔	✔	✔	Berries appear in summer and ripen to black in fall.	Northeast, partial Midwest
Black-eyed Susan (*Rudbeckia fulgida*)	24 to 30 inches tall and 12 to 24 inches wide	Average, well-drained soil	Full sun to part shade	5-9	✔			Late blooming with seeds feeding birds post-bloom into winter.	Northeast, partial Midwest
Spotted Bee Balm (*Monarda punctata*)	6 to 36 inches tall	Dry, sandy soil	Full sun	4-9	✔			Hummingbirds are attracted to flowers. Caterpillars feed on foliage and stems. (Can spread.)	Northeast, partial Midwest, South, Southwest
Anise Hyssop (*Agastache foeniculum*)	3 to 5 feet tall	Prefers moist but will tolerate dry soil	Full to part sun	4-8	✔			Flowers attract hummingbirds and seeds attract goldfinches.	Midwest
Northwind Switch Grass (*Panicum virgatum* 'Northwind')	5 feet tall and 2 feet wide	Average soil moisture	Full sun, part sun	3-9		✔	✔	Provides winter cover for songbirds.	Throughout U.S. except Pacific Ocean coastline
Common Sneezeweed (*Helenium autumnale*)	3 to 5 feet tall and 3 feet wide	Wet to moist soil	Sun to part sun	3-9	✔			Flowers begin in late summer and continue into fall.	All
Eastern Redbud (*Cercis canadensis*)	12 to 25 feet	Moist soil	Full sun	4-9	✔			Pink flowers in spring.	Northeast, Southeast, partial Midwest
Western Redbud (*Cercis occidentalis*)	8 to 20 feet	Dry, well-drained soil	Full sun	7-9	✔			Redbud choice for drier soils in the western U.S.	West, partial Southwest

Plant name	Plant size	Water needs	Preferred lighting conditions	Hardy to (USDA zones)	Provides			Main season of interest	Native range
					🌼	🌲	🏺		
Compass Plant (*Silphium laciniatum*)	Up to 8 feet tall	Moist, rich soil	Full to partial sun	3-9	✓			Yellow blooms begin in summer and last through early fall. The leaves will usually orient themselves on a north-south axis.	Midwest
Cup Plant (*Silphium perfoliatum*)	Up to 6 feet tall	Medium to wet soil	Full to partial sun	4-8	✓			Yellow blooms begin in late summer. Plant leaves form "cups" which hold water.	Northeast, some Midwest, some Southeast, some Southwest
Red Bee Balm (*Monarda didyma*)	24 to 48 inches tall	Well-drained soil	Full sun to part sun	4-9	✓			Scarlet red flowers attract hummingbirds.	Northeast, some Midwest, some Southeast
Purple Coneflower (*Echinacea purpurea*)	2 to 4 feet tall and 2 feet wide	Dry, well-drained soil	Full sun to part shade	4-9	✓			Blooms early summer through fall, produces seeds for birds. Also attractive to butterflies and native bees.	Midwest, some Southeast, Northeast
False Mesquite/ Fairy Duster (*Calliandra eriophylla*)	1 to 3 feet tall and 3 feet wide	Sandy soil	Full sun	9-11	✓			Purple and pink flowers provide food for hummingbirds in late winter and spring.	West
Red Fairy Duster (*Calliandra californica*)	5 feet tall and wide	Loam, rocky soil	Full sun to light shade	9-11	✓			Red flowers attract hummingbirds.	West
Cardinal Flower (*Lobelia cardinalis*)	1 to 6 feet tall	Moist soil	Sun to part shade	2-8	✓			Flowers are specialized for feeding hummingbirds.	Northeast, Southwest, Midwest, some Southwest
Blue Vervain (*Verbena hastata*)	2 to 5 feet tall and 1 to 2.5 feet wide	Average to wet soil	Full sun to part shade	3-8	✓			Seeds are attractive to cardinals, sparrows, and juncos.	Throughout U.S.
Pink Tickseed (*Coreopsis rosea*)	1 to 2 feet tall	Medium moisture, well-drained, sandy soil	Full sun	3-8	✓			Can spread in areas with ideal growing conditions. Birds eat the seeds.	Northeast, Southeast
Gray Goldenrod (*Solidago nemoralis*)	1 to 2 feet tall	Dry to medium, well-drained soil	Full sun	3-9	✓			Can spread in areas with ideal growing conditions. Attracts bees and butterflies. Seeds feed birds.	Northeast, Southwest, partial West, Southeast

Deer-resistant garden

While there are deer deterrents such as bitter sprays and fencing, the easiest way to have a garden that the deer will not eat is to fill it with plants they do not find palatable. The native plants featured here grow well in a full sun location—with either dry or moist soil.

Butterfly Milkweed (*Asclepias tuberosa*) brings bright orange flowers to the garden bed that will attract a variety of insects and butterflies—in addition to hummingbirds—that will feed from its flowers. Grow it in front of a taller shrub, such as Sweet Pepperbush (*Clethra alnifolia*), that produces flowers that attracts hummingbirds. As the seed pods mature, expect a new host of avian visitors to enjoy the spoils, including robins, goldfinches, and warblers.

American Goldfinches will be very attracted to the seedheads of a variety of *Rudbeckia* species interplanted in the deer-resistant garden. These tough plants bloom for long periods in the summer. Pair these perennials with Big Bluestem (*Andropogon gerardii*) to provide cover for birds and seasonal interest from fall into winter.

For an evergreen that will provide food for birds throughout the winter, consider adding Eastern Red Cedar (*Juniperus virginiana*) to the back of the garden. These large trees can reach up to 40 feet in height over their lifetime, and the blue cones (that look like berries) will attract Cedar Waxwings and Eastern Bluebirds. Birds such as chickadees and kinglets will eat the insects that the evergreen attracts. The tree is also used for nesting by thrashers, sparrows, and the Eastern Towhee. Cultivars of *Juniperus virginiana* may offer smaller size plants. Deer tend to leave this evergreen alone due to the bitter taste in its needles, but it will bounce back if the deer do sample it in very bad winters. This plant is dioecious, so you will need at least one male and one female plant to produce the blue fruit.

Planting deer-resistant native plants together in one location will encourage deer to keep on moving. Shown here is a newly planted garden, in which the perennials will fill in the empty spaces in the coming growing seasons.

The berries of sumac will feed American Robins in the winter.

A combination of Purple Coneflower (*Echinacea purpurea*), Black-eyed Susan (*Rudbeckia hirta*), and Wild Quinine (*Parthenium integrifolium*) is unpalatable to deer.

Many varieties of Helianthus are deer-resistant. Grosbeaks and finches will seek out the seeds of sunflowers.

Great Coneflower (*Rudbeckia maxima*) blooms will produce large seedheads that goldfinches and chickadees will eat from.

A Song Sparrow sings from its perch atop an Eastern Red Cedar (*Juniperus virginiana*).

Blanket Flower (*Gaillardia* spp.) will attract native bees and other pollinators. The seedheads will later feed finches.

Butterfly Milkweed (*Asclepias tuberosa*) begins blooming in early summer. In the background is Sweet Pepperbush (*Clethra alnifolia*), before it begins to bloom.

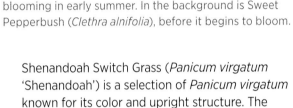

The blue cones of Eastern Red Cedar (*Juniperus virginiana*) are attractive to many birds.

Shenandoah Switch Grass (*Panicum virgatum* 'Shenandoah') is a selection of *Panicum virgatum* known for its color and upright structure. The straight species, also known as Wand Panic Grass, will spread and can be used for screening portions of the garden. It pairs well when grown behind Black-eyed Susans (*Rudbeckia* spp.), Smooth Oxeye (*Heliopsis helianthoides*), or Rattlesnake Master (*Eryngium yuccifolium*).

BIRDS ATTRACTED

 Crows, Magpies & Jays

 New World Sparrows

 Woodpeckers

 Chickadees & Titmice

 Finches

 Cardinals, Grosbeaks & Buntings

 Nuthatches

 Waxwings

 Mockingbirds & Thrashers

 Blackbirds & Orioles

 Wood Warblers

 Thrushes

 Wrens

 Vireos

 Hummingbirds

CONSIDER THE FOLLOWING NATIVE PLANTS FOR DEER-RESISTANCE

Plant name	Plant size	Water needs	Preferred lighting conditions	Hardy to (USDA zones)	Provides			Main season of interest	Native range
					✿	🌲	🦅		
Big Bluestem (*Andropogon gerardii*)	4 to 8 feet tall	Moist soil	Full sun to light shade	3-8	✓	✓	✓	Green/blue green foliage turns russet red in winter. Seedheads form beginning in August.	Northeast, Midwest, partial Southeast
Great Coneflower (*Rudbeckia maxima*)	5 to 7 feet tall	Average, moist well-drained soil	Full sun	5-9	✓			Yellow flowers bloom in summer with raised center cones, that later provide food for birds.	Midwest, some Southwest
Smooth Oxeye (*Heliopsis helianthoides*)	2 to 6 feet tall	Moist, well-drained soils	Full sun to part shade	3-9	✓			Yellow flowers bloom July through September, later producing seed.	Northeast, Southeast, Midwest, partial Southwest
Shenandoah Switch Grass (*Panicum virgatum* 'Shenandoah')	3 to 4 feet tall and 18 to 24 inches wide	Dry to wet	Full sun to partial shade	4-9	✓	✓	✓	Red color in fall with small red flower plumes. Fall and winter interest. Hosts native caterpillars and provides food for birds.	Northeast, Southeast, Midwest, Southwest, partial West
Wand Panic Grass (*Panicum virgatum*)	3 to 6 feet tall	Dry to moist soil	Full sun to partial shade	5-9	✓	✓	✓	Attractive to butterflies. Provides cover, food and nesting material for ground-feeding and game birds.	Northeast, Southeast, Midwest, Southwest, partial West
Purple Coneflower (*Echinacea purpurea*)	2 to 4 feet tall and 2 feet wide	Dry, well-drained soil	Full sun to part shade	4-9	✓			Blooms early summer through fall, produce seeds for birds. Also attractive to butterflies and native bees.	Midwest, some Southeast, Northeast
Blanketflower (*Gaillardia aristata*)	1 to 3 feet tall	Average to dry soil. Drought-tolerant once established	Full sun	3-8	✓			Begins blooming in June and blooms throughout the summer, producing seed for birds later in the season.	West, Southwest, partial Midwest, partial Northeast.

Plant name	Plant size	Water needs	Preferred lighting conditions	Hardy to (USDA zones)	Provides			Main season of interest	Native range
					🌸	🌲			
Star Tickseed (*Coreopsis pubescens*)	2 to 4 feet tall and up to 2.5 feet wide	Average to dry, well-drained soil	Sun to part sun	5-9	●			Blooms early summer into October, producing seedheads for birds to eat late in the season.	Southeast, partial Southwest, partial Midwest
Wild Quinine (*Parthenium integrifolium*)	3 to 5 feet tall	Dry to medium soil	Full sun	4-8	●			Host plant for moths and butterflies.	Midwest, Northeast, partial Southeast.
Culver's Root (*Veronicastrum virginicum*)	2 to 6 feet tall	Moist, well-drained soil.	Full sun to part shade	3-8	●			Flowers throughout summer attract hummingbirds.	Northeast, partial Midwest
Rattlesnake Master (*Eryngium yuccifolium*)	Up to 4 feet tall	Medium wet to medium dry soil	Full sun	4-9	●			Attractive to many pollinators and seeds later feed birds.	Southeast, partial Southwest, partial Midwest
Swamp Sunflower (*Helianthus angustifolius*)	3 to 10 feet tall and 2 to 4 feet wide	Moist to wet	Sun	5-9	●			Maturing seedheads will feed birds. Plants will spread so start with one.	Southeast, partial Northeast, partial Southwest
Black-eyed Susan (*Rudbeckia hirta*)	1 to 2 feet tall	Moist to dry, well-drained soil	Sun	3-7	●			Birds are attracted to seeds.	Northeast, Southeast, Midwest, West, some Southwest
Butterfly Milkweed (*Asclepias tuberosa*)	1 to 3 feet tall	Dry to moist soil	Full sun	3-9	●			Host plant for butterfly species such as the monarch. Hummingbirds feed from orange flowers.	Northeast, Southeast, Midwest, partial Southwest
Sweet Pepperbush (*Clethra alnifolia*)	3 to 8 feet tall and 4 to 6 feet wide	Moist to wet soil	Full sun to part shade	3-9	●			Blooms in late summer, attracting hummingbirds, Birds eat the seed.	Southeast, partial Northeast
Swamp Milkweed (*Asclepias incarnata*)	3 to 5 feet tall and 1 to 2 feet wide	Moist, medium to wet clay soil.	Part sun to sun	3-9	●			Flowers will attract hummingbirds. Also host plant for monarch butterflies.	Southeast, parts of Northeast, Southwest, Midwest

Continued on next page

Plant name	Plant size	Water needs	Preferred lighting conditions	Hardy to (USDA zones)	Provides 🌼 🌲 🪺	Main season of interest	Native range
Bush Honeysuckle (*Diervilla lonicera*)	2 to 3 feet tall and 2 to 5 feet wide	Dry to moist soil	Full sun to part shade	3-7	✓ ✓ ✓	Yellow flowers attract hummingbirds. Dry fruit feeds songbirds in the fall. Colorful foliage in landscape. Two or more shrubs are recommended.	Northeast, partial Midwest, partial Southeast
Bayberry (*Morella pensylvanica*)	5 to 8 feet tall	Adaptable to sandy or clay soils	Full to part sun	2-9	✓ ✓	Berries attract birds and will provide shelter for birds when grown as a hedge.	Northeast, Southeast
Deergrass (*Muhlenbergia rigens*)	Up to 6 feet tall	Average to dry, well-drained soil.	Full sun to light shade	7-10	✓ ✓ ✓	Attracts birds and butterflies. Foliage ranges from silver-green to purple in color.	West, Southwest
Common Sneezeweed (*Helenium autumnale*)	3 to 5 feet tall and 3 feet wide	Wet to moist soil	Sun to part sun	3-9	✓	Flowers begin in late summer and continue into fall.	All
Short Toothed Mountain Mint (*Pycnanthemum muticum*)	24 to 26 inches tall and wide	Moist soil	Full sun to part shade	4-8	✓ ✓	Attracts and feeds many insects, which in turn provides food for birds.	Northeast
Pennsylvania Sedge (*Carex pensylvanica*)	8 to 10 inches tall and 12 to 18 inches wide	Well-drained to dry soil	Sun to shade	3-6	✓ ✓	Larval host plant for insects. Seeds attract birds.	Northeast, Midwest
Spotted Bee Balm (*Monarda punctata*)	6 to 36 inches tall	Dry, sandy soils	Full sun	4-9	✓	Hummingbirds are attracted to flowers. Caterpillars feed on foliage and stems. (Can spread.)	Northeast, partial Midwest, South, Southwest

Plant name	Plant size	Water needs	Preferred lighting conditions	Hardy to (USDA zones)	Provides ❀ 🌲 🪹			Main season of interest	Native range
Eastern Red Cedar (*Juniperus virginiana*)*	Up to 40 feet tall	Average, dry to moist well-drained soil	Part sun to sun	3-9	✓	✓	✓	Blue cones attract a variety of birds in the winter.	Southeast, Midwest, Northeast
Little Bluestem (*Schizachyrium scoparium*)	18 to 24 inches tall and 12 inches wide	Low	Sun to part shade	3-9	✓	✓	✓	Color changes from blue green to red in fall into winter. Will spread in larger landscapes. Seeds feed birds. 'Standing Ovation' is a compact cultivar.	Northeast, Midwest, West, Southwest, Southeast
Fragrant Sumac (*Rhus aromatica*)	6 to 12 feet tall	Dry to moist soil	Full sun to shade	3-9	✓	✓		Colorful fall foliage. Thickets provide cover for birds. American Robins and flickers will eat seeds in winter.	Partial West, Northeast, Midwest, Southwest, Southeast
Compass Plant (*Silphium laciniatum*)	Up to 8 feet tall	Moist, rich soil	Full to partial sun	3-9	✓			Yellow blooms begin in summer and last through early fall. The leaves will usually orient themselves on a north-south axis (hence the common name of this plant).	Midwest
Cup Plant (*Silphium perfoliatum*)	Up to 6 feet tall	Medium to wet soil	Full to partial sun	4-8	✓			Yellow blooms begin in late summer. Plant leaves form "cups" which hold water.	Northeast, some Midwest, some Southeast, some Southwest

*This native plant can be invasive in some parts of the U.S. so make sure to check if it is recommended for your area first.

Southwest retreat

Xeriscaping is the practice of landscaping with plants that use limited water throughout the growing seasons, using eco-friendly methods. In extremely arid areas, cacti are paired with stones to create a landscape that covers the soil to prevent moisture loss. In other growing areas, native plants with similar water needs are planted together to replace large sections of lawn, which uses an abundance of water each year to maintain and contributes to the draw on resources from limited areas such as rivers and streams.

Gardens in the Southwest and Western United States are ideal locales for this due to the average yearly rainfall, but xeric growing practices can be implemented anywhere individuals prefer to use less water in their landscape.

Native plants in the xeric zone are ideal for use in hot, dry, south- and west-facing areas of the property, and are also beneficial to pollinators such as hummingbirds.

BIRDS ATTRACTED

 Hummingbirds

 New World Sparrows

 Blackbirds & Orioles

 Wood Warblers

 Mockingbirds & Thrashers

 Vireos

 Waxwings

 Chickadees & Titmice

 Cardinals, Grosbeaks & Buntings

 Woodpeckers

 Thrushes

 Kinglets

 Wrens

Gardens can incorporate xeric regions and areas of plants that require a bit more water to succeed. These plants can be incorporated into garden plans as "bands" or swaths, by grouping plants with the sameWater needs together.

Six of the plants provide a steady food source for hummingbirds, beginning with Rocky Mountain Penstemon (*Penstemon strictus*), Wild Bergamot (*Monarda fistulosa*) and Arizona Red Columbine (*Aquilegia desertorum*). At the height of the summer, the California Fuchsia (*Epilobium canum*) steals the show with bright scarlet flowers that are 1 to 2 inches long and are very attractive to hummingbirds. This perennial plant is native to California's foothills and coastal areas. Many of the plants are also host plants for several moths and butterflies.

The Desert Olive (*Forestiera pubescens*) provides a privacy screen and can be left as a shrub or pruned into a multi-stemmed small tree with twisty branches. Two plants are needed (male and female) in order to produce the fruit. This is planted near the lower-growing California Fuchsia since it shares similar light and soil moisture requirements.

Black-headed Grosbeaks have a rich warble similar to that of a robin, but is sweeter and faster.

California Poppy (*Eschscholzia californica*) is easy to grow from seed and can create large swaths of flowers for a colorful display. Watering throughout the growing season will extend its blooming period.

PLANTS FEATURED IN ILLUSTRATION:

Ⓐ Arizona honeysuckle
(*Lonicera arizonica*)

Ⓑ Wild Bergamot
(*Monarda fistulosa*)

Ⓒ Arizona Red Columbine
(*Aquilegia desertorum*)

Ⓓ Golden Columbine
(*Aquilegia chrysantha*)

Ⓔ Rocky Mountain Penstemon
(*Penstemon strictus*)

Ⓕ California Poppy
(*Eschscholzia californica*)

Ⓖ California Fuchsia
(*Epilobium canum*)

Ⓗ Desert Olive/Stretchberry
(*Forestiera pubescens*)

THIS SOUTHWEST RETREAT PLAN FEATURES THE FOLLOWING NATIVE PLANTS

Plant name	Plant size	Water needs	Preferred lighting conditions	Hardy to (USDA zones)	Provides ✿ ♠ 🥣			Main season of interest	Native range
California Fuchsia (*Epilobium canum*)	1 to 3 feet tall and up to 4 feet wide	Low, drought-tolerant but needs supplemental water in desert locale	Full sun	7a-10b	✓			Red tubular flowers from June through October.	West, Southwest
Desert Olive / Stretchberry (*Forestiera pubescens*)	5 to 10 feet tall	Well-draining, occasionally moist, drought-tolerant	Full sun to partial shade	7a-10b	✓	✓	✓	Flowers in March and April. Fruit in July through September. Leaves turn yellow in the fall.	West, Southwest
Rocky Mountain Penstemon (*Penstemon strictus*)	1 to 3 feet tall	Coarse, well-draining soil	Full sun	4a-9b	✓			Blue-purple flowers from May to July.	West
Arizona Honeysuckle (*Lonicera arizonica*)	Can climb to 15 feet	Coarse, well-draining soil	Full sun	5a-9b	✓			Red-orange flowers trumpet shaped.	Southwest
Golden Columbine (*Aquilegia chrysantha*)	1 to 3 feet tall	Sandy to loamy, moist well-drained soil	Full sun to partial shade	3b-9b	✓			Yellow flowers April through September.	Southwest, partial West
Arizona Red Columbine (*Aquilegia desertorum*)	1 to 2 feet tall	Moist, well-draining soil.	Full sun to partial shade	5a – 8b	✓			Red and yellow flowers July through September.	Southwest, partial West
Wild Bergamot (*Monarda fistulosa*)	3 to 4 feet tall	Dry to moist, well-draining soil	Full sun to partial shade	3a-8b	✓			Lavender flowers from June through August that attract hummingbirds.	Southwest, Southeast, Midwest, Northeast, partial West
California Poppy (*Eschscholzia californica*)	1 to 2 feet tall	Well-draining, drought-tolerant	Full sun	3b-9b	✓			Flowers March through May but extended bloom with added water.	West, Southwest

YOU CAN ALSO CONSIDER THE FOLLOWING PLANTS

Plant name	Plant size	Water needs	Preferred lighting conditions	Hardy to (USDA zones)	Provides 🌸 🌲🌲 🪺			Main season of interest	Native range
Purple Sage (*Salvia dorrii*)	1 to 3 feet tall and wide	Dry, rocky soils	Full sun	5-9	✓			Purple flowers attract hummingbirds in late spring through late summer.	West
Eastwood's Manzanita (*Arctostaphylos glandulosa*)	Up to 8 feet	Dry, gravely soil	Full sun to part shade	8-10	✓			White to pink flowers in January to March, followed by reddish-brown berries.	West
Chuparosa (*Justicia californica*)	6 feet tall and wide	Well-drained, drought-tolerant	Full sun	8-10	✓			Tubular flowers in red or yellow bloom spring through fall.	Partial West, partial Southwest

Golden Columbine (*Aquilegia chrysantha*) provides flowers April through September for hummingbirds.

Rocky Mountain Penstemon (*Penstemon strictus*) adds a blue-purple blossom to the garden and is attractive to hummingbirds.

Jason Kitting

📍 ALBUQUERQUE, NEW MEXICO

"As a kid growing up in the mountains east of Albuquerque, I had no idea we had any brightly colored birds. I thought we only had little brown birds," he explained. "One Christmas, I was given a birdbath and about a week later, the first flock of Western Bluebirds showed up. I was completely amazed by the brilliant blues and reds of the males and had to find out what these birds were."

Jason Kitting pauses during a birdwatching outing in Albuquerque, New Mexico. The brightly colored Western Bluebird was the first bird that caught Jason Kitting's eye.

Luckily, Jason's dad had a bird book which Jason used to identify the birds. "From then on, I was hooked. Soon after I put up a birdhouse, and the Western Bluebirds were my first tenants!"

Jason lives in a major migratory pathway for many birds entering and leaving the Rocky Mountains and the far northwestern corner of North America. In addition, there is a high diversity of habitat types in a small area of land.

"Albuquerque is located in central New Mexico, with the Rio Grande River flowing right through the middle, a dry grassland to the west, and the Sandia and Manzano Mountains to the east," he said. "You can go from low elevation riparian habitat (about 5,000 feet) along the river, and then up to the top of the Sandia Mountains (10,600 feet) in cold spruce/fir forest in less than an hour's drive."

Jason works with several different birds thanks to his involvement with both Rio Grande Bird Research and the Wildlife Rescue Inc. of New Mexico. With the Rio Grande organization, Jason helps with long-term bird banding projects—which provides data on habitat use and population trends of western birds during different seasons of the year.

In addition to educating the public through the social media accounts of both organizations, Jason also participates in community education opportunities for both children and adults. Through programs such as raptors at schools, bird festivals, summer camps, and other outdoor events, Jason is able to share information on native birds and other wildlife. "We also share the many human-caused challenges these creatures now face, in order to increase public knowledge and encourage people to make changes that will benefit the birds."

On Jason's property, availability of fresh water is one of the main ways he draws birds in for a visit. "Since I'm located in a desert, water is a good way to bring everyone in, even if they are species that don't typically visit feeders."

Jason provides a variety of feeders (seed, suet, and sugar water) in combination with native plants. "I like to mix flowers, shrubs, and grasses when I can so that seed/berries, nectar, and shelter are available for as much of the year as possible." He includes the Rocky Mountain Bee Plant (*Cleome serrulata*) in his garden, which provides a long bloom period and is drought-hardy. "The warblers love to go after the insects on the stems of the plants, and the seed pods produce **a lot** of seeds which winter birds go nuts over," Jason said.

Birdwatching, either in the garden or in the New Mexico area, has helped Jason to understand and appreciate nature as a whole. "By learning more about the birds, I have learned so much about their habitat requirements, food sources, yearly cycles—which has introduced me to other passions and interests I probably never would have discovered. I always like to tell people that the best part of birding is the beautiful places you get to see while chasing the birds!"

A Western Bluebird perches on top Yerba santa (*Eriodictyon californicum*).

Flowering vines hideaway

Having a dedicated area outside to admire birds and support vining natives can be a positive addition to different sized gardens—whether you only have a small balcony or a large plot of land.

Creating an enclosure that allows the honeysuckle to twine around will also provide you with cover to birdwatch in the garden. A simple hideaway is creating a corner trellis configuration, using lattice panels from home improvement stores. These can be anchored together with brackets to form an L-shape. Make sure to anchor the trellis into the ground by attaching it to rebar or stakes. Native vines can grow up the sides of the trellis, either in fabric grow bags or directly into the soil. If you would rather purchase an arbor, look for one that is sturdy and will provide additional support with anchors.

The bloom period for Crossvine (*Bignonia caproolata*) is late spring through early summer, but can be intermingled with an annual vine to provide continuous flowering throughout the growing seasons. This one is best grown in a container to control its spread.

Many of the native varieties of flowering vines also have non-native, and sometimes invasive, counterparts. *Wisteria frutescens* (such as the 'Amethyst Falls' cultivar) provides a native alternative to the non-native and often invasive *Wisteria sinensis* (Chinese Wisteria). The flowers are more compact than the non-native variety, but the vine is generally better behaved. To keep it maintained, it can be pruned in the spring. The pea-shaped flowers attract hummingbirds and the vine also provides cover for birds to hide in.

Another native vine that has a non-native look alike is Virgin's Bower Clematis (*Clematis virginiana*). The non-native Sweet Autumn Clematis (*Clematis paniculata*) grows rapidly and self-seeds easily. The two are commonly confused but can be

The purple blooms of native Wisteria (*Wisteria frutescens*) blooms in late spring to early summer.

A Ruby-throated Hummingbird approaches a native honeysuckle flower.

BIRDS ATTRACTED

Hummingbirds

New World Sparrows

Thrushes

Woodpeckers

differentiated by their leaves. The native clematis has jagged edges while the non-native has rounded leaves.

Trumpet Honeysuckle (*Lonicera sempervirens*) does best when provided with a structure for it to climb. Orange Honeysuckle (*Lonicera cilosa*) is another native option. It will grow with a trellis or use nearby shrubs and trees as a support. The flowers will also attract bees and butterflies in addition to hummingbirds, and birds such as robins, finches, and thrushes will eat the fruit later in the season. Both are substitutes for the aggressive and invasive Japanese Honeysuckle (*Lonicera japonica*).

Trumpet Honeysuckle (*Lonicera sempervirens*) can be grown along a trellis or arbor.

RECOMMENDED PLANTS FOR A FLOWERING VINE HIDEAWAY

✿ = Food 🌲 = Cover 🪺 = Nesting Material/Site

Plant name	Plant size	Water needs	Preferred lighting conditions	Hardy to (USDA zones)	Provides			Main season of interest	Native range
					✿	🌲	🪺		
Trumpet Honeysuckle (*Lonicera sempervirens*)	Up to 15 feet tall	Moist, well-drained soil	Full sun to shade	4-9	✓		✓	Hummingbirds visit red flowers and songbirds eat red berries.	Southeast
Orange Honeysuckle (*Lonicera cilosa*)	10 to 20 feet tall	Moist to dry soil	Partial shade	4-9	✓		✓	A honeysuckle that does well in partly shaded areas and features bright orange flowers. Fruits will feed songbirds.	West
Crossvine (*Bignonia capreolata*)	5 to 20 feet tall and up to 50 feet if allowed	Rich, well-drained soil	Part sun to sun	5-9	✓			Hummingbirds enjoy the red-orange-yellow flowers in late spring through early summer.	Southeast, lower Midwest
Amethyst Falls Wisteria (*Wisteria frutescens* 'Amethyst Falls')	25 to 30 feet tall	Moist, well-drained soil	Sun	5-9	✓	✓		Purple flowers attract hummingbirds in the late spring.	South
Virgin's Bower Clematis (*Clematis virginiana*)	10 to 20 feet tall and 3 to 6 feet wide	Average to wet, well-drained soil	Part sun to shade	3-9	✓		✓	Flowers are attractive to hummingbirds. Birds eat the seeds. Foliage provides covers and nesting sites for finches and Indigo Buntings.	Northeast, Southeast, partial Midwest

Woodland retreat

Woodland habitats excel at creating different levels of plantings which will appeal to a variety of species: plants that grow close to the ground, perennials, shrubs and tall trees. Birds such as the Chipping Sparrow will take advantage of all three layers when looking for food and picking a suitable nesting site.

Using native plants to make wooded areas hospitable for woodpeckers puts the focus on trees that will attract them. Leaving snags for birds to nest in and search for food will encourage them to stay. Incorporating understory trees, such as Allegheny Serviceberry (*Amelanchier laevis*) and Flowering Dogwood (*Cornus florida*), provide food sources for other varieties of birds as well. *Cornus spp.* also provide nesting opportunities for Bell's Vireo and the Summer Tanager (Adams 2013).

Pagoda Dogwood (*Cornus alternifolia*) is another *Cornus* species that produces fruit attractive to birds, such as Brown Thrashers. It is easy to grow and prefers to be in a spot protected from wind. In addition to the fruit, the flowers provide food for bees and butterflies in the spring, and the small tree provides pleasant landscape architecture in the winter.

Flowering Dogwood (*Cornus florida*) is a great understory tree for garden edges and in woodland habitats.

Pagoda Dogwood (*Cornus alternifolia*) blooms in the spring, which provides food for native bees and butterflies. The flowers ripen to fruit that will feed birds later in the growing season.

Black Haw Viburnum (*Viburnum prunifolium*) will spread by suckers in the wild, but can be kept smaller with pruning. This shrub will produce olive-shaped fruits that ripen to deep blue-black in color and has burgundy-red foliage in the fall (a nice alternative to the invasive Burning Bush, which is usually planted for the red leaves in autumn).

An additional native shrub to consider—that provides food, nesting areas and cover—is the Black Huckleberry (*Gaylussacia baccata*). When given space, the plant will spread to form a thicket, and the purple-black berries are attractive to many birds. It's also pollinator-friendly, with both native bees and butterflies seeking out its nectar.

A Pileated Woodpecker scales an older tree looking for insects.

BIRDS ATTRACTED

 Thrushes

 Hummingbirds

 Woodpeckers

 Wood Warblers

 Finches

 Mockingbirds & Thrashers

 Chickadees & Titmice

 Vireos

 New World Sparrows

 Bushtits

 Swifts

 Tyrant Flycatchers

 Owls

Smooth Solomon's-Seal (*Polygonatum biflorum*) is commonly used in shaded gardens for its foliage and white flowers. In the fall, the plant produces blue berries that feed a variety of thrushes. Birds also feast on the insects that feed on the plant. This is a good understory plant in a woodland setting.

Black Haw Viburnum (*Viburnum prunifolium*) blooms in early spring in the Northeast. The large shrub will later produce fruit that will attract many species of birds.

A Red-shafted Northern Flicker
excavating a tree for nesting.

FOCUS ON TREES

Eastern Cottonwood (*Populus deltoides*) can reach heights of 80 to 100 feet and is often used by woodpeckers for nest sites due to its soft wood (Kress 1985). The largest living woodpecker in North America, the Pileated Woodpecker, will chisel rectangular holes into rotted trees in order to find carpenter ant nests.

Paper Birch (*Betula papyrifera*) is native to the northern United States, and birds such as the Black-capped Chickadee, Common Redpoll, Pine Siskin, and Fox Sparrow are attracted to the catkins. The peeling bark of the tree is used by Philadelphia Vireos, Black-throated Green Warblers, and even Red-shouldered Hawks for nests. Yellow-bellied Sapsuckers will drill holes in the tree to extract sap. Hummingbirds will even make use of these "sapwells," also feeding on the sap.

Swamp White Oak (*Quercus bicolor*) is a tree that will grow tall or will spread out—depending on the available space. It will do well in wetter areas, and tolerates compacted soil. This tree will attract many insects—such as leafhoppers, beetles, Hairstreak butterflies, and a variety of moths. The acorns are an important food source for woodpeckers (as well as Wood Ducks and Ruffled Grouse).

Another large oak tree to consider including is the Red Oak (*Quercus rubra*), which provides cavities for woodpeckers, as well as bats and tree squirrels. It is a food source for many insects and the acorns also provide food for Wood Ducks and Wild Turkeys.

The American Sycamore (*Platanus occidentalis*) is a fast-growing large tree that produces fuzzy "fruit" that stays on the tree throughout the winter. It contains many seeds that birds will feast on. It is a long-lived tree (up to 250 years!) and is best suited in a large space where it will be able to spread out. Very old giant trees can reach 75 feet high and have hollow trunks that can reach 15 feet in diameter, and can provide homes to Chimney Swifts, Pileated Woodpeckers, Barred Owls, Great Crested Flycatchers, Wood Ducks, and even raccoons and sometimes black bears.

Signs of rectangular holes in trees show that a Pileated Woodpecker has been previously excavating for a meal.

Northern Red Oak with fall color.

While Paper Birch (*Betula papyrifera*) is a short-lived tree. It is popular to include in gardens for the peeling white bark. The Black-capped Chickadee will eat the catkins and Yellow-bellied Sapsuckers will drill holes to feed on the tree sap.

According to the North American Breeding Bird Survey, Northern Flicker population numbers have decreased 47 percent between 1966 and 2019. Leaving dead trees on the property (as long as it is not a safety hazard) will be beneficial to birds such as Northern Flickers (both Red-shafted in the West and Yellow-shafted in the East). These birds excavate holes in the wood for cavities to nest inside, usually 6 to 15 feet above the ground. Northern Flickers will often target dead or diseased tree trunks or large branches for excavation. They may reuse the same cavity in a following year, or another spot created by another species, according to The Cornell Lab of Ornithology.

Along the western coast, consider incorporating Oceanspray (*Holodiscus discolor*) into an open woodland garden. It is a trifecta plant that offers food, cover, and nesting opportunities for a variety of birds, including Bushtits. The large plumes of white flowers make it an excellent native substitute for Butterfly Bush (*Buddleja davidii*), which is a noted invasive species in many regions.

Tiger Lilies (*Lilium columbianum*) can be grown at the edge of woodland gardens, and prefers moist areas in sun to partial shade. The bright orange flowers are attractive to hummingbirds.

A Northern Flicker pauses on a birdbath to drink water.

American Goldfinches are one of the many birds that will feast on the seeds of American Sycamore (*Platanus occidentalis*) in the winter months. Other birds that enjoy the seeds include Dark-eyed Juncos, Black-capped Chickadees, and Purple Finches.

Oceanspray (*Holodiscus discolor*) blooms from May through August.

A Sapsucker on a tree in the fall.

Plant name	Plant size	Water needs	Preferred lighting conditions	Hardy to (USDA zones)	Provides			Main season of interest	Native range
					🌸	🌲	🪺		
Allegheny Serviceberry/ Shadblow (*Amelanchier laevis*)	15 to 25 feet tall and wide	Medium moist well-drained soil	Part sun/ shade	4-8	✓			Birds will eat the purple-black fruit in late summer. Leaves provide red autumn color.	Midwest and Northeast
Flowering Dogwood (*Cornus florida*)	20 to 40 feet tall	Dry to moist soil	Part shade to shade	5-9	✓			Early spring flowers develop into red berries relished by birds.	Northeast, Southeast, partial Southwest
Smooth Solomon's-Seal (*Polygonatum biflorum*)	4 to 5 feet tall and 2 feet wide	Dry to moist soil	Part sun to full shade	3-8	✓			Flowers attract birds, including hummingbirds. Many birds are attracted to insects that feed on the plant as well as the blue berries in fall.	Northeast, Midwest, Southeast, partial Southwest, partial West
Pinxterbloom Azalea (*Rhododendron periclymenoides*)	6 to 10 feet tall and 4 to 6 feet wide	Moist, well-drained and acidic soil	Part shade to part sun	4-9	✓			Large clusters of tubular flowers in white, pink, or purple will attract hummingbirds.	Southeast, Northeast
Oceanspray (*Holodiscus discolor*)	8 to 16 feet tall and wide	Moist to dry soil	Sun to part shade	4b-9b	✓	✓	✓	Insects provide food for Bushtits. Seeds are eaten by songbirds.	West, partial Southwest
Tiger Lilies (*Lilium columbianum*)	2 to 3 feet tall and 10 to 18 inches wide	Moist, well-drained soil	Sun to part shade	4-9	✓			Flowers in late spring to early summer and provides food for hummingbirds.	West
Black Haw Viburnum (*Viburnum prunifolium*)	8 to 15 feet tall and 6 to 15 feet wide	Moist to dry soil	Sun to light shade	4-9	✓			Produces attractive white flowers in spring that will turn into blue-black fruits that feed birds.	Northeast, Southwest
Pagoda Dogwood (*Cornus alternifolia*)	15 to 25 feet tall and 20 to 30 feet wide	Moist, well-drained soil but tolerates dry spots	Full sun to part shade	3-7	✓			Provides four-season interest and berries for birds.	Northeast, Southeast, some Midwest

Plant name	Plant size	Water needs	Preferred lighting conditions	Hardy to (USDA zones)	Provides			Main season of interest	Native range
Swamp White Oak (*Quercus bicolor*)	Up to 60 feet tall and 20 to 30 feet wide	Medium to wet soil	Full sun to part shade	3-8	✓	✓	✓	Attracts several insects and acorns feed woodpeckers.	Northeast, Midwest
Red Oak (*Quercus rubra*)	Up to 75 feet tall	Medium-wet to medium-dry soil	Full sun to shade	3-7	✓	✓	✓	Provides cavities for woodpeckers and is a host to several insects.	Northeast, partial Southeast, partial Midwest
Arrowwood Viburnum (*Viburnum dentatum*)	6 to 10 feet tall and wide	Average, well-drained soil	Full sun to part shade	2-8	✓	✓		Blue-black, berry-like drupes in late summer and early fall attract birds.	Southeast, Northeast

ADDITIONAL NATIVE PLANTS

Plant name	Plant size	Water needs	Preferred lighting conditions	Hardy to (USDA zones)	Provides			Main season of interest	Native range
American Sycamore (*Platanus occidentalis*)	75 feet high and up to 15 feet wide trunks	Moist soil	Full sun	4-9	✓	✓	✓	Birds eat the seed in winter months. Hollow trunks provide nesting sites for woodpeckers and owls.	Northeast, Southeast, partial Midwest
Black Huckleberry (*Gaylussacia baccata*)	1 to 3 feet tall and wide	Dry to wet, but acidic soil	Full sun to part shade	3-7	✓	✓	✓	Birds will eat berries. Mockingbirds and catbirds use it for nesting. Turkey and quail use it for cover.	Northeast, Southeast, partial Midwest
Paper Birch (*Betula papyrifera*)	50 to 70 feet tall and up to 35 feet wide	Well-drained soil	Part shade to full sun	1-5	✓	✓	✓	Decorative peeling bark is used by some birds for nests. Catkins are a source of food for many birds.	Northeast, partial Midwest, partial West

Create an owl-friendly habitat

Similar to other species of songbirds, habitat loss is a threat for many owls. North America hosts nineteen owl species—most are nocturnal (meaning they are active at night).

Where you live will factor into the type of habitat you can offer owls. Barred Owls, Great Horned Owls, and Eastern Screech-Owls live in forests. Barn Owls are found in grasslands and Western Screech-Owls are found in open woodlands.

Living in a rural setting or quiet suburb with access to open, grassy areas to hunt in and lots of trees to perch in, is an ideal environment to host owls, as opposed to an urban environment. This type of setting provides a safe area that is free from construction sites, busy roads, or industrial areas, which can be dangerous for owls. Nearby farms should also not use pesticides or herbicides. According to The Cornell Lab of Ornithology, planting hedgerows alongside roads can help prevent Barn Owls from being hit by vehicles as they fly low over fields to hunt.

Fast facts

- Great Horned Owls are found throughout the Americas.

- Snowy Owls will migrate from the Arctic, and can sometimes be found along east coast beaches in the winter or open areas across the mid-continent.

- Barn Owls will nest in holes in trees and in structures such as barn lofts, church steeples, and nest boxes.

- Ten species of owls will nest in cavities excavated by woodpeckers.

- Barred Owls are monogamous and will often reuse nests.

Owls look for natural cavities to nest in, like this Great Grey Owl.

Leaving dead trees, or snags, on the property will be welcoming to owls. (Trees that may fall and damage houses, cars, or people will have to be removed for safety reasons.) Barred Owls are one species that will look for natural cavities to nest in, about 20 to 40 feet high, in a large tree. Broken-topped trees and cavities are their preferred nest sites. They will also repurpose stick nests of other birds and use nest boxes (Bannick 2008).

Eastern Screech-Owls however will repurpose tree holes that were opened or enlarged by woodpeckers (including abandoned nest holes), fungus, rot, or squirrels. One tree that is likely to host the Eastern Screech-Owl is Eastern Red Cedar (*Juniperus virginiana*). Northern Saw-whet Owls may also use this tree for nesting or roosting.

Another tree that provides an attractive nesting site for screech-owls is the Bur Oak (*Quercus macrocarpa*). This large tree provides cavities that are perfect for screech-owls, and because of its broad limbs, this tree is also a favored nesting site for Blue-gray Gnatcatchers, Summer Tanagers, and Yellow-throated Vireos.

American Beech (*Fagus grandifolia*) can reach 40 to 70 feet tall at full maturity, and the nut crop provides food for at least twenty-five bird species. It is also a nesting site for Great Horned Owls.

Great Gray Owls will nest on top of broken snags, in a site near an opening in the forest, such as within a meadow, bog, or field. They are found both in Canada and the Northwest and Northeast U.S. In the U.S., they will seek out pine and fir forests adjacent to montane meadows (a seasonally moist to waterlogged soil area found in valleys, flats, and gentle slopes) between 2,500 and 7,500 feet. Out west (California and Oregon) during the winter months, Great Gray Owls will move into oak woodlands and lower elevation mixed deciduous and evergreen forests to nest.

Brush piles on the property will help to entice mice and other small rodents to hide inside—which will provide food for owls. Brush piles should be situated away from homes and outbuildings.

Shrubs have many uses

Did you know? Using shrubs to mark property borders aids in privacy and provides cover and nesting opportunities for all birds. The narrowest part of the shrub border between the property line and the lawn should be at least 8 feet wide (Adams 2013).

BIRDS ATTRACTED

 Owls

 Woodpeckers

 Cardinals, Grosbeaks & Buntings

 Vireos

 Wood Warblers

 Gnatcatchers

Be a responsible land owner

One of the best things you can do to help owl populations survive and even flourish is to not use rat or mouse poison on the property. If vermin are an issue, using spring-loaded mouse and rat traps are the best (and most humane) solution to remove unwanted populations. When poison is consumed by a mouse or rat, the animal will not die right away, still serving as bait to hungry owls. An owl might also pick up a deceased mouse or rat found in the woods or in a garden that could have consumed the poison. In both cases, this will also poison and often kill the owl (or any other raptor that consumes the rodent).

ILLUSTRATION FEATURES THE FOLLOWING

A American Beech (*Fagus grandifolia*)

B Eastern Red Cedar (*Juniperus virginiana*)

C Snag (dead tree for nesting opportunities)

D Eastern cottonwood (*Populus deltoides*)

E Bur Oak (*Quercus macrocarpa*)

F Brush pile

Pin Oak (*Quercus palustris*) does well in areas with acidic soil. The tree's acorns are eaten by many songbirds, in addition to wild turkeys and ducks.

The American Beech (*Fagus grandifolia*) tends to hold on to its brown leaves throughout the winter, which provides space for insects to lay eggs. Check trees in spring as the larvae begin to hatch and attract songbirds such as the Worm-eating Warbler.

After the deciduous trees have dropped their leaves it becomes easier to spot owls in the trees at night. This mixed tree line of conifers and deciduous trees that borders a grassy area for hunting is attractive to owls.

NATIVE TREES TO CREATE AN OWL-FRIENDLY HABITAT

Plant name	Plant size	Water needs	Preferred lighting conditions	Hardy to (USDA zones)	Provides			Main season of interest	Native range
					🌸 Food	🌲 Cover	🪺 Nest		
Eastern Cottonwood (*Populus deltoides*)	80 to 100 feet	Moist to well-drained soil	Full sun	3-9			✓	Provides nesting areas for Great Horned Owls.	Northeast, Midwest, Southwest
American Beech (*Fagus grandifolia*)	50 to 70 feet	Moist, well-drained soil	Full sun	4-9	✓		✓	Provides nesting areas for Great Horned Owls and nuts for other birds.	Northeast, Southeast, partial Midwest
Eastern Red Cedar (*Juniperus virginiana*)*	Up to 40 feet tall	Average, dry to moist well-drained soil	Part sun to sun	3-9	✓	✓	✓	Blue cones attract a variety of birds in the winter.	Southeast, Midwest, Northeast
Bur Oak (*Quercus macrocarpa*)	Up to 80 feet tall and 20 to 30 feet wide	Medium to dry soil	Full to partial sun	3-8	✓	✓	✓	Produces large acorns and is a source plant for several types of Hairstreak butterfly caterpillars. Good nesting site for birds and owls.	Midwest
American Sycamore (*Platanus occidentalis*)	75 feet high and up to 15 feet wide trunks	Moist soil	Full sun	4-9	✓	✓	✓	Birds eat the seed in winter. Hollow trunks provide nesting sites for woodpeckers and owls.	Northeast, Southeast, partial Midwest
Douglas-fir (*Pseudotsuga menziesii*)	15 to 100 feet tall	Moist soil	Full sun to partial shade	5-6	✓	✓	✓	Fast-growing evergreen that provides food. Also provides cover for Northern Spotted Owls.	West
Blue Spruce (*Picea pungens*)	50 to 75 feet tall and 10 to 20 feet wide	Moist, well-drained soil	Full sun	2-7	✓	✓	✓	Provides cover for owls. Provides food for siskins, nuthatches, and crossbills.	West
Pin Oak (*Quercus palustris*)	50 to 70 feet tall and 25 to 40 feet wide	Wet, loamy acidic soil. Tolerates other conditions	Full sun	4-8	✓	✓	✓	A tree for long-term planning. It will begin to produce acorns when it is between 15 and 20 years old.	Northeast, partial Midwest
Western Hemlock (*Tsuga heterophylla*)	50 to 150 feet tall and 25 to 30 feet wide	Moist, acidic, well-drained soil	Sun to shade	4-9	✓	✓	✓	Woodpeckers nest in cavities in mature or dead trees. Owls utilize natural cavities. Seeds also feed many birds.	West

*This native plant can be invasive in some parts of the U.S. so make sure to check if it is recommended for your area first.

Warbler-friendly habitat

When aiming to attract the elusive warblers to a garden space, the focus turns to many of the native plants and trees that host several insect species. Warblers are often not seen at bird feeders and prefer to stay hidden in the shrubbery.

Warblers are some of the smallest birds—weighing under an ounce and usually less than 6 inches long. Their main source of food is insects, and they prefer to hunt for them in treetops of mature forests. Providing different layers of habitat/plants on your property is important, so large parcels of private land are ideal to be converted into warbler-friendly territory. You'll also support a wide-range of other songbirds, too.

The Black-throated Green Warbler breeds mainly in coniferous and mixed forests, and will nest around spruce, white pine, hemlock, red cedar, and jack pine.

There are fifty-four species of warblers, and half of them are migratory. They will spend summers in North America and will migrate to subtropical or tropical climates during the winter. You may have a warbler pass through your garden during the spring or fall migration as a stopover point. Some warblers will feast on berries as well.

In your large space, focus on including trees—such as spruce which host the Spruce Budworm, a favorite of the Cape May Warbler. Also include shrubs to increase your chances of at least hearing them somewhere on your property. There are a variety of willows (*Salix spp.*) that are native throughout the United States and are a popular food and nesting source for birds, but be sure to plant them away from drainage lines since the roots will seek out moisture and can cause damage.

Yellow Warblers will seek out nesting sites in willows, blueberry, and elderberry shrubs when grown in thickets. Birds such as the Chestnut-sided Warbler and the Common Yellowthroat will nest in relatively small areas of an acre or more (Kress 2006), so consider incorporating a variety of shrubs into the garden space.

When creating a habitat that will entice them to linger, consider the multiple levels of plantings. Warblers will spend a lot of their time in the shrub and tree layer. Fallen trees are beneficial too if they are left to decompose back into the ground because they are home to several insects, including termites. On a warm spring day, termites can hatch, which will attract warblers to eat—and make it easier for you to spot them, too.

A Chestnut-sided Warbler perches within the spring growth of Riverbank Grape (*Vitis riparia*). This warbler breeds in areas with large shrubs and trees, and also does well in disturbed habitats. The green and scented flowers of the Riverbank Grape attract many insects, which attract insectivorous birds such as this warbler.

There are several native trees to choose from that will host insects that will attract warblers. One large tree that is native to a significant portion of the United States is the Sugar Maple (*Acer saccharum*), which is popularly known for its sap which is boiled into maple syrup. This tree will grow fairly large over time (60 to 75 feet at full maturity) and offers food and shelter to a variety of birds. The insects attracted to the early spring leaves will feed warblers, kinglets, vireos, Scarlet Tanagers and Yellow-bellied Sapsuckers. In the fall, the winged seeds will feed grosbeaks, Pine Siskins, goldfinches, and nuthatches. The tree also provides nesting accommodations for orioles, woodpeckers, flickers, and cardinals.

Hackberry (*Celtis occidentalis*) is a large canopy tree that is attractive to warblers, and also supports more than thirty species of moths and butterflies. Many bird species will also eat the fruit, including Mountain Bluebird, Cedar Waxwings, and American Robins. Oak trees (*Quercus* spp.) are also beneficial in attracting the insects that warblers eat. Oaks host more than 550 species of butterfly and moth caterpillars, as well as other insects that birds eat, including ants, bees, beetles, aphids, sawflies, and leafhoppers. In spring, the catkins on oak trees will attract warblers to feast on wasps, caterpillars, and aphids, which are attracted to the catkins. (Learn about why oaks are so great on page 18.)

A Northern Flicker will hunt for ants along the ground, often blending into the surroundings.

A young oak tree will take time to grow but will be a great investment. It is a keystone plant, a term that entomologist Doug Tallamy coined to signify a native plant's importance in the food chain.

Many warblers are migratory birds

Did you know? Four warblers are neotropical migrants that spend most of their lives "wintering" in Central or South America.

- The Hooded Warbler migrates to Central America and parts of the Caribbean.
- The non-breeding range of the Black-and-White Warbler extends from Mexico to northern South America and the Caribbean.
- The Magnolia Warbler flies to Central America and the Caribbean.
- The Kentucky Warbler winters from Mexico to northern South America, and the Caribbean.

Most Blackburnian Warblers will spend winter in South America. When it is present in North America, it will feed mostly in treetops, searching along small branches and twigs.

The Common Yellowthroat is the only warbler that will nest in open marshes, and is found throughout the United States.

BIRDS ATTRACTED

 Wood Warblers

 Nuthatches

 Thrushes

 Finches

 Chickadees & Titmice

 Crows, Magpies & Jays

 Woodpeckers

 Mockingbirds & Thrashers

 Wrens

 Blackbirds & Orioles

 Waxwings

 Cardinals, Grosbeaks & Buntings

 Vireos

 New World Sparrows

 Hummingbirds

THE FOLLOWING NATIVE PLANTS HELP CREATE AN APPEALING HABITAT FOR WARBLERS

Plant name	Plant size	Water needs	Preferred lighting conditions	Hardy to (USDA zones)	Provides			Main season of interest	Native range
Sugar Maple (*Acer saccharum*)	60 to 75 feet tall and 40 to 50 feet wide	Rich, moist, well-drained soil	Full sun to part shade	3-8	✓	✓	✓	Autumn provides brightly colored red, yellow, or orange leaves for landscape appeal. Sap can be collected and boiled to create maple syrup.	Northeast, part of the Midwest
Red Maple (*Acer rubrum*)	40 to 60 feet tall and 40 feet wide	Moist, well-drained soil	Full sun to part shade	3-9	✓	✓	✓	Yellow to bright red autumn color.	Northeast, Midwest, Southeast, part of Southwest
Willow (*Salix* spp.)	Average 20 to 30 feet tall depending on variety	Moist soil	Full sun to part shade	3-9	✓	✓		Catkins appear in early spring. Host plant for several butterflies. Works well in wet areas, but keep away from drainage pipes.	Throughout U.S. (depending on species)
Hackberry (*Celtis occidentalis*)	40 to 60 feet tall and wide	Wet, medium to dry soil	Full sun	3-9	✓	✓		Provides spring nectar for hummingbirds. Birds will eat the berries.	Northeast, part Midwest
Paper Birch (*Betula papyrifera*)	50 to 70 feet tall and up to 35 feet wide	Well-drained soil	Part shade to full sun	1-5	✓	✓	✓	Decorative peeling bark is used by some birds for nests. Catkins are a source of food for many birds.	Northeast, partial Midwest, partial West
Blue Spruce (*Picea pungens*)	50 to 75 feet tall	Moist soil	Full sun	1-7	✓	✓	✓	Provides food and shelter for siskins, nuthatches, and crossbills. Insects attract warblers.	West
Swamp White Oak (*Quercus bicolor*)	Up to 60 feet tall and 20 to 30 feet wide	Medium to wet soil	Full sun to part shade	3-8	✓	✓	✓	Attracts several insects. Acorns feed woodpeckers.	Northeast, partial Midwest

Plant name	Plant size	Water needs	Preferred lighting conditions	Hardy to (USDA zones)	Provides			Main season of interest	Native range
Red Oak (*Quercus rubra*)	Up to 75 feet tall	Medium-wet to medium-dry soil	Full sun to shade	3-7	✓	✓	✓	Provides cavities for woodpeckers and is a host to several insects.	Northeast, partial Midwest, partial Southeast
Eastern Red Cedar* (*Juniperus virginiana*)	Up to 40 feet tall	Average, dry to moist well-drained soil	Part sun to sun	3-9	✓	✓	✓	Blue cones attract a variety of birds in the winter.	Southeast, Midwest, Northeast
Sumac (*Rhus* spp.)	9 to 15 feet tall	Average, dry to moist soil	Full sun to part shade	3-9	✓	✓		Provides fruit in winter. Will spread, so give it space or use to stabilize a slope.	Throughout U.S.
Red Elderberry (*Sambucus racemosa*)	8 to 18 feet tall and up to 10 feet wide	Moist, loamy soil	Full sun to shade	3-9	✓	✓	✓	Flowers attract hummingbirds. Red fruit is attractive to birds. When grown in thickets, is attractive nesting site for the Yellow Warbler.	West, partial Midwest

*This native plant can be invasive in some parts of the U.S. so make sure to check if it is recommended for your area first.

The Golden-crowned Kinglet favors dense coniferous forests, especially those of spruce, fir, and hemlock. It will feed on a wide variety of insects and will often hang upside down from tips of twigs as it seeks food.

Laura Jackson

⦿ EVERETT, PENNSYLVANIA

Growing up, Laura Jackson would explore the woods on her family's dairy farm where she would regularly encounter birds. Her parents, also bird enthusiasts, nurtured Laura's interest.

Her passion and advocacy for birds continued as she grew older, and she met her future husband, Mike, in an ornithology class that was part of a summer travel study program. "My commitment to bird conservation is one reason why I taught environmental science and biology for over thirty years," she said.

Laura also serves on the Executive Board of the Pennsylvania Audubon Council and spearheads the Bird-Friendly Blooms program for her local chapter.

"Knowing that we've lost over 3 billion birds since 1970, mostly because humans have destroyed or poisoned natural habitats, keeps me committed to protecting natural habitats, reducing the impact of climate change, and educating others about the importance of native habitats—especially forests."

Laura uses her private property to offer a wide variety of native species that provide food and cover throughout the seasons. She and her husband live on the lower area of Tussey Mountain in Pennsylvania, which is part of the Ridge-and-Valley Appalachians. "Our 120-acre property is part of an extensive block

Laura Jackson plants a tree seedling as part of a volunteer conservation project sponsored by the Pennsylvania Society for Ornithology.

Spring is Laura's favorite season, because of the returning migrants to her property, such as this Rose-breasted Grosbeak in an Eastern Redbud tree (*Cercis canadensis*).

One of the wildflower meadows in September on the Jackson property. About three acres of fallow farm fields have been transformed into native wildflower meadows.

A pair of Wood Ducks return each spring to nest in the box above the small woodland pond.

(about 9,000 acres) of intact oak-hickory forest where Scarlet Tanagers, Wood Thrush, and a variety of warblers proliferate. Living immersed in nature offers a unique perspective since birds and other wildlife are all around our home."

To provide water, Laura and Mike built a small woodland pond and five shallow impoundments near the woods, which attract many birds. Closer to the house, there is a recirculating shallow water garden and two bubbling boulders, as well as a heated birdbath in the winter.

"We also like to supplement the natural foods with bird seed, hummingbird nectar, suet cakes, peanuts, plus grape jelly for orioles and orange halves for orioles and woodpeckers," she said. "We feed year-round, but don't feed when black bears become frequent visitors to our backyard."

"Mike and I have landscaped the areas around our house as a bird sanctuary, planting many species of native flowers, shrubs, and trees. We have reduced our lawn (and mowing) by planting native wildflower meadows below our house."

Mike builds birdhouses for their property, which are used by Eastern Bluebirds, Tree Swallows, Black-capped Chickadees, and White-breasted Nuthatches. Larger boxes are nesting places for screech-Owls and Wood Ducks.

Many of the plantings are protected by a 5-foot fence around the 5 closest acres surrounding their home, which keeps out deer. She has included many winterberry hollies, serviceberries, and crabapples in her plantings, since the fruit attracts a variety of birds, especially in fall and winter. She's also incorporated oak trees because of their role as an important food source for almost a thousand different caterpillar species—critical food for baby birds.

Coastal garden for migrating birds

Many of the birds that use North America's coastlines for migration and habitat have different needs than species found further inland. Providing native plants that help birds fuel up during migration stopover points along the coastlines will help them migrate successfully. Goldenrod is one of the best native plants to include in the garden for its ability to host and feed several insects, which in turn provides food for birds.

Climate change is one of the reasons for habitat decline, and it is especially seen along coastlines. A scientific study published in Scientific Reports (2019) examined fifty years of results from the U.S. Geological Survey Breeding Bird Surveys found that higher temperatures and less precipitation has reduced waterbird habitat, negatively affecting the number of birds in the Great Basin area. This region, which includes land in Nevada, Oregon, Utah, California, Idaho, and Wyoming, is a major part of the Pacific Flyway, a major migration route along the west coast for birds. (See page 28 for more information on migration routes.) The warmer temperatures can make wetlands saltier—which is a stressor for young waterbirds—or causes the water to evaporate, meaning the birds need to travel further for fresh water sources. The study was one of the first to show a direct link between climate change having an effect on water quality.

High salt content in the water also plays a role in plants' abilities to adapt and flourish along coastlines, so include native plants that have a higher salt tolerance. Switchgrass (*Panicum virgatum*) can be incorporated into a coastal garden due to its salt tolerance. It also aids with erosion control. Two pine trees to consider (depending on which coastline is closest) are Shortleaf Pine (*Pinus echinata*) or Shore Pine (*Pinus contorta* subsp. *latifolia*). Both are salt-tolerant and are great substitutes for non-native pine trees. Bushtits, kinglets, chickadees, and woodpeckers will feed on the insects that hide on the branches and in the cones.

A Willow Flycatcher perches within a tall shrub as it forages for insects, such as wasps, bees, winged ants, beetles, flies, caterpillars, and moths.

A Shortleaf Pine (*Pinus echinata*)

Native to the Atlantic coastline, consider incorporating Northern Bayberry (*Morella pensylvanica*) and Inkberry (*Ilex glabra*) in your garden plan. Both will do very well along the coastline. When planted in groups, the shrubs will form coverage for birds to hide in. They can be interplanted to form a hedgerow or planted individually. Both Bayberry and Inkberry are dioecious species, meaning that one plant is female and one is male. In order to get fruit on the female plants to feed the birds into the winter, you will need a male plant nearby for pollination.

Northern Bayberry (*Morella pensylvanica* (syn. *Myrica pensylvanica*)) is a shrub that provides multiple benefits for birds. Female plants will produce waxy gray fruit that feed Tree Swallows during their fall migration and is a favorite of Yellow-rumped Warblers. The berries that remain on the shrub throughout the winter are also consumed by songbirds such as American Robins, Brown Thrashers, catbirds, Cedar Waxwings, chickadees, crows, Eastern Bluebirds, meadowlarks, mockingbirds, Northern Flickers, Tree Swallows, Tufted Titmice, wrens, and Red-bellied Woodpeckers. The leaves remain on the shrubs which also provides winter shelter for birds.

Along the Pacific coastline, consider the easy-to-grow California Coffeeberry (*Frangula californica*), which can also be grown together as a mass to form a hedge. The flowers attract hummingbirds and native bees in the spring, and later the plant offers berries that California Towhees, Spotted Towhees, robins, and thrashers adore. This is also a dioecious species, so you'll need a male and female plant.

Lemonade Berry (*Rhus integrifolia*) is an important wildlife plant that is hardy and grows along the southern California coast. Bushtits will eat the fruit, and the branches provide nesting opportunities for other birds.

A Song Sparrow uses Eastern Red Cedar (*Juniperus virginiana*) for scouting and coverage.

A Pine Warbler perches inside Northern Bayberry (*Morella pensylvanica*) for cover. This species feeds primarily on insects, seeds, and berries, but will also visit bird feeders for suet and other items.

Lemonade Berry (*Rhus integrifolia*), found along the southern California coastline, produces tart berries that birds eat.

NATIVE PLANTS TO CREATE A COASTAL GARDEN FOR MIGRATING BIRDS

Plant name	Plant size	Water needs	Preferred lighting conditions	Hardy to (USDA zones)	Provides			Main season of interest	Native range
Seaside Goldenrod (*Solidago sempervirens*)	1 to 6 feet tall and about 2 feet wide	Average water needs, salt-tolerant	Full sun	5-10	✓			Yellow flowers in fall. Plant does not spread by rhizomes.	Northeast, Southeast
Northern Bayberry (*Morella pensylvanica* (syn. *Myrica pensylvanica*))	5 to 8 feet tall	Adaptable to sandy or clay soils	Full to part sun	2-9	✓	✓		Berries attract birds and will provide shelter for birds when grown as a hedge.	Northeast, partial Southeast
Inkberry (*Ilex glabra*)	5 to 8 feet	Adaptable to all soils	Full sun to full shade	3-7	✓	✓		Songbirds eat berries produced in the fall.	Northeast
California Coffeeberry (*Frangula californica*)	5 to 10 feet tall and wide	Well-draining soil	Full sun to part shade	8-9	✓	✓	✓	Berries turn red, purple, and then black as the summer season progresses. Birds will also eat insects attracted to this plant.	West
Lemonade Berry (*Rhus integrifolia*)	3 to 30 feet tall and 2 to 20 feet wide	Well-drained soil	Sun to part shade	9-11	✓	✓	✓	Bushtits will eat the berries. Provides nesting and shelter.	West
Wand Panic Grass (*Panicum virgatum*)	3 to 6 feet tall	Dry to moist soil	Full sun to partial shade	5-9	✓	✓	✓	Attractive to butterflies. Provides cover, food, and nesting material for ground-feeding and game birds.	Northeast, Southeast, Midwest, Southwest, partial West
Sweet Pepperbush (*Clethra alnifolia*)	3 to 8 feet tall and 4 to 6 feet wide	Moist to wet soil	Full sun to part shade	3-9	✓			Blooms in late summer, attracting hummingbirds, Birds eat the seed.	Southeast, partial Northeast
Coastal Red Cedar (*Juniperus virginiana* var. *silicicola*)	Up to 40 feet	Sand, well-draining	Full sun	7-11	✓	✓		Cinnamon red bark provides winter interest. Can also provide a windbreak due to size.	Southeast

Plant name	Plant size	Water needs	Preferred lighting conditions	Hardy to (USDA zones)	Provides			Main season of interest	Native range
					✿	🌲	🪹		
Beach Blanket flower (*Gaillardia pulchella*)	1.5 to 2 feet tall	Sandy, well-draining soil	Full sun	2-11	✓			Highly drought and salt tolerant. Seedheads attract goldfinches.	Southeast
Shortleaf Pine (*Pinus echinata*)	50 to 100 feet tall	Dry to medium soil	Full sun	6-9	✓	✓	✓	Provides winter cover. Birds eat the seeds and larvae that use the tree as a host plant.	Southeast
Shore Pine (*Pinus contorta* subsp. *latifolia*)	33 to 115 feet tall	Well-drained soil	Full sun	6-8	✓	✓	✓	Seeds eaten by crossbills, chickadees, mourning doves, jays, nuthatches, finches, and siskins.	West

BIRDS ATTRACTED

- Chickadees & Titmice
- Vireos
- Cardinals, Grosbeaks & Buntings
- New World Sparrows
- Blackbirds & Orioles
- Nuthatches
- Creepers
- Waxwings
- Finches
- Woodpeckers
- Crows, Magpies & Jays
- Wood Warblers
- Hummingbirds
- Swallows
- Thrushes
- Mockingbirds & Thrashers
- Wrens
- Tyrant Flycatchers
- Pigeons & Doves
- Hawks & Eagles
- Falcons
- Bushtits

Streamside garden

Birds are more likely to seek out shallow areas of water surrounded by rocks—not in wide open areas. Combining that with the sounds of moving water makes streams great spaces to attract birds. Incorporating native plants that will thrive in a moisture-rich landscape—where the water level can change depending on the seasonal rainfall—will also provide shelter and a food source for a variety of birds.

Sweet Pepperbush (*Clethra alnifolia*) is a great choice for naturalizing along the streamside, ideally providing privacy because it will grow into thickets. Silky Dogwood (*Cornus amomum*) will also grow thickly if given the chance, but is effective for erosion control.

A Mourning Dove pair on a rock in a stream.

BIRDS ATTRACTED

 Hummingbirds

 Cardinals, Grosbeaks & Buntings

 Chickadees & Titmice

New World Sparrows

Thrushes

 Wood Warblers

 Wrens

 Crows, Magpies & Jays

 Blackbirds & Orioles

 Nuthatches

 Vireos

 Mockingbirds & Thrashers

 Waxwings

 Woodpeckers

 Finches

 Swifts

Black Willow (*Salix nigra*) makes an excellent native plant for growing along a streamside garden because it is also flood resistant. The shallow root system helps with erosion control, but it is a fast-growing deciduous tree and needs space. It's a host plant to several butterfly and moth species (providing food for birds) and provides nesting crooks for birds such as hummingbirds and warblers.

River Birch (*Betula nigra*) is a multi-stemmed tree that offers yellow foliage in the fall and peeling bark along the trunks in the winter months. The tree attracts many insects, which birds use to feed their young. Many adult songbirds will also eat the catkins in the spring, including Redpolls and Pine Siskins.

Native flowering plants also brighten stream edges. The native habitat for Cardinal Flower (*Lobelia cardinalis*) is wet soil along streams, swamps, and wet woods. Tall Swamp Marigold (*Bidens coronata*) is an annual that grows around marshes, ditches, and woodland areas. The yellow flowers bloom late in the season and will self-seed. Joe Pye Weed, (*Eutrochium maculatum*), which favors moist soil, will attract several pollinators when the flowers are in bloom. When the plants go to seed in autumn, they will attract finches to feed.

The catkins of the River Birch (*Betula nigra*) are a favorite among Purple Finches, Black-capped Chickadees, Pine Siskins, and White-winged Crossbills. It also provides landscape interest with peeling bark.

Swamp Marigold (*Bidens coronata*) will self-seed in moist or wet soil.

Cardinal Flower (*Lobelia cardinalis*) features bright red flowers along 8 inch long flower stems (also known as terminal spikes).

THE FOLLOWING NATIVE PLANTS WOULD GROW WELL ALONG A STREAM

Plant name	Plant size	Water needs	Preferred lighting conditions	Hardy to (USDA zones)	Provides			Main season of interest	Native range
					🌼	🌲	🌰		
Gray Dogwood (*Cornus racemosa*)	6 to 16 feet tall	Prefers moist soil but will adapt to drier sites	Full sun, part sun, part shade	4-8	✓		✓	White fruit appears in fall against red stems. Good source for caterpillars.	Northeast, Southeast, Midwest
Sweet Pepperbush (*Clethra alnifolia*)	3 to 8 feet tall and 4 to 6 feet wide	Moist to wet soil	Full sun to part shade	3-9	✓			Blooms in late summer, attracting hummingbirds. Birds eat the seed.	Southeast, partial Northeast
Silky Dogwood (*Cornus amomum*)	10 feet tall and wide	Well-drained to wet soil	Full sun to part shade	4-8	✓			Blue fruit attracts a variety of songbirds, along with Wild Turkey and Wood Duck.	Eastern
Buttonbush (*Cephalanthus occidentalis*)	6 to 12 feet or taller	Wet soil	Part shade to shade	5-9	✓			Seeds are attractive to ducks and shorebirds. Very popular with insects for nectar. Hummingbirds will also feed on flowers.	Northeast, Southeast, some Southwest
Joe Pye Weed (*Eutrochium maculatum*, formerly *Eupatorium purpureum*)	Up to 7 feet tall (although there are several shorter cultivars) and 2 to 3 feet wide	Moist soil	Full sun	3-8	✓	✓		Flowers are attractive to hummingbirds and finches will eat the seeds. Host plant for 40+ butterfly and moth larvae.	Northeast, Southeast, Midwest
River Oats Sea Oats (*Chasmanthium latifolium*)	2 to 3 feet tall and 1 to 2 feet wide	Moist soil	Part sun to part shade	5-8	✓		✓	Birds eat the seedheads and use the leaves for nesting materials. Can self-sow, but can be removed easily when young. Provides winter interest and can help with erosion control.	Southeast, partial Southwest, partial Northeast
Black Willow (*Salix nigra*)	30 to 60 feet tall	Wet soil	Full sun to part shade	2-8	✓	✓	✓	This fast-growing plant will grow into a tree when given enough room. Provides food, cover, and nesting area for birds.	Northeast, Southeast, some western

Plant name	Plant size	Water needs	Preferred lighting conditions	Hardy to (USDA zones)	Provides			Main season of interest	Native range
					🌼	🌲🌲	🪺		
Tiger Lilies (*Lilium columbianum*)	2 to 3 feet tall and 10 to 18 inches wide	Moist, well-drained soil	Sun to part shade	4-9	✓			Flowers in late spring to early summer and provides food for hummingbirds.	West
Cardinal Flower (*Lobelia cardinalis*)	1 to 6 feet tall	Moist	Sun to part shade	2-8	✓			Flowers are specialized for feeding hummingbirds.	Northeast, Southwest, Midwest, some Southwest
Swamp Marigold (*Bidens coronata*)	2 to 4 feet tall	Medium to wet soil	Full sun	3-8	✓			Seeds are attractive to Swamp Sparrows, Purple Finches, and Common Redpolls.	Northeast, Southeast, partial Midwest
River Birch (*Betula nigra*)	Up to 80 feet tall at maturity	Wed to medium soil	Sun to part sun	4-9	✓	✓	✓	Attracts many insects which birds use to feed their young during nesting season. Some songbirds will also eat the catkins.	Southeast, partial Midwest

In autumn, Joe Pye Weed (*Eutrochium maculatum*) will attract finches to feed.

Savannah Sparrow in a red maple tree.

Mountain habitat

A combination of native plants and trees offer shelter and food to a variety of birds that call the higher elevations home. Several pine trees are a valuable food source for the birds in the mountainous area, with at least fifty-four bird species eating pine seeds (Kress 1985). Clark's Nutcrackers, which reside in forest habitats in the mountains of the western United States, will excavate large seeds from pine cones, which they then stash in a pouch under their tongue and carry away to bury for the winter. Nutcrackers are champions at burying pine seeds (sometimes tens of thousands) in hidden caches in fall, then re-finding them during winter.

The Mountain Chickadee is found in coniferous mountain forests made up of pine, spruce, fir or Douglas Fir, and groves of aspen. It often feeds high in the trees, gleaning food from twigs and seeking out insect eggs and pupae, as well as spiders and their eggs. It will also eat many seeds (including those from pine trees), some berries, and small fruits.

For dry areas, consider incorporating Western Juniper (*Juniperus occidentalis*), which is an important food source for Pinyon Jays, Townsend's Solitaires, Clark's Nutcrackers, Cedar Waxwings, and American Robins.

The plant species highlighted in this illustration features evergreen trees (Douglas Firs and Western White Pines)—both which provide food, cover, and nesting areas for birds. The Douglas Fir is fast growing and the Western White Pine works well in large garden spaces.

Smaller, spring-blooming trees of Serviceberry (*Amelanchier alnifolia*) and American Plum (*Prunus americana*) provide early season flowering and fruit later in the season for birds. These two smaller trees are paired with the Cascade Mountain Ash (*Sorbus scopulina*), which also produces white flowers but is followed by orange-red berries that persist throughout fall and winter. Another option is planting Silver Buffalo-Berry (*Shepherdia argentea*), which offers red fruit and is extremely cold-hardy. This fruit-bearing border provides a varied selection for thrushes, mockingbirds and thrashers, waxwings, cardinals and grosbeaks, and orioles. The rest of the selected plants include bright-colored perennial flowers of various heights and ornamental grass, all of which will go to seed in fall and provide food for a variety of bird species. The flowers look best in groupings of three to five, interspersed together to form large swaths of color. If space is limited, plants in this plan can be omitted (such as one Rudbeckia variety instead of two).

Chickadees & Titmice

 Crows, Magpies & Jays

 Vireos

 New World Sparrows

 Woodpeckers

 Cardinals, Grosbeaks & Buntings

 Waxwings

 Wrens

 Blackbirds & Orioles

 Wood Warblers

 Mockingbirds & Thrashers

 Nuthatches

 Thrushes

 Hummingbirds

A Green-Head Coneflower (*Rudbeckia laciniata*).

Although Clark's Nutcrackers often live in remote areas, you may encounter them at picnic grounds and scenic-view parking lots. They have a remarkable memory which allows them to locate their seed caches into late winter.

ILLUSTRATION FEATURES THE FOLLOWING

A Western White Pine
(*Pinus monticola*)

B American Plum
(*Prunus americana*)

C Black-eyed Susan
(*Rudbeckia hirta*)

D Cascade Mountain Ash
(*Sorbus scopulina*)

E Douglas Fir
(*Pseudotsuga menziesii*)

F Freshwater Cord Grass
(*Spartina pectinata*)

G Green-Head Coneflower
(*Rudbeckia laciniata*)

H Northern Mule's-Ears
(*Wyethia amplexicaulis*)

I Red-Spike Mexican Hat
(*Ratibida columnifera*)

J Saskatoon Serviceberry
(*Amelanchier alnifolia*)

K Silver Buffalo-Berry
(*Shepherdia argentea*)

L Wand Panic Grass
(*Panicum virgatum*)

M Nuttall's Sunflower
(*Helianthus nuttallii*)

THIS MOUNTAIN HABITAT PLAN FEATURES THE FOLLOWING NATIVE PLANTS

Plant name	Plant size	Water needs	Preferred lighting conditions	Hardy to (USDA zones)	Provides			Main season of interest	Native range
					✿	▲▲	☘		
Western White Pine (*Pinus monticola*)	90 to 150 feet tall	Rich/moist drained soil	Sun	3-6	✓			One of the most important seed providers for birds in the region.	West (mountains)
American Plum (*Prunus americana*)	Up to 35 feet tall	Moist, rich well-drained soil	Full sun to shade	3-8	✓			Flowers bloom in April and May, followed by bright red fruit that feeds many birds in August and September.	Midwest, partial Southeast, partial Northeast
Black-eyed Susan (*Rudbeckia hirta*)	1 to 2 feet tall	Moist to dry, well-drained soil	Sun	3-7	✓			Birds are attracted to seeds.	Northeast, Southeast, Midwest, West, some Southwest
Cascade Mountain Ash (*Sorbus scopulina*)	Up to 12 feet tall	Moist, rich soil	Full sun to shade	2-8	✓			Orange-red berries feed birds in fall through winter.	West, partial Southwest
Douglas Fir (*Pseudotsuga menziesii*)	15 to 100 feet tall	Moist soil	Full sun to partial shade	5-6	✓	✓	✓	Fast-growing evergreen that provides food and cover. Western Tanagers will use as a nesting habitat.	West
Freshwater Cord Grass (*Spartina pectinata*)	5 to 6 feet tall	Moist to wet rich soil	Full sun	4-9	✓			Stiff seedheads attract birds in fall. Will spread, so not suitable for small areas.	West, Southwest, partial Southeast
Green-Head Coneflower (*Rudbeckia laciniata*)	3 to 12 feet tall	Moist soil	Full sun to shade	4-9	✓			Flowers bloom from July through October and then develop into brown seedheads.	Midwest, Northeast, Southeast, Southwest, partial West
Northern Mule's-Ears (*Wyethia amplexicaulis*)	1 to 3 feet tall	Moist to wet soil	Full sun	4-9		✓	✓	Yellow flowers in late spring to early summer.	West

Plant name	Plant size	Water needs	Preferred lighting conditions	Hardy to (USDA zones)	Provides			Main season of interest	Native range
					🌼	🌲	🪹		
Red-Spike Mexican Hat (*Ratibida columnifera*)	3 feet tall	Dry to moist, well-drained soil	Full sun	4-9	✓			Flower heads produce seeds for birds.	Midwest, partial Southwest
Saskatoon Serviceberry (*Amelanchier alnifolia*)	4 to 18 feet tall	Dry, rocky soil	Full sun	4-8	✓			Small purple fruits will feed birds.	West, partial Midwest
Silver Buffalo-Berry (*Shepherdia argentea*)	Up to 20 feet tall	Dry to moist soil	Full sun	3-9	✓			Low-maintenance shrub that produces red berries.	West
Wand Panic Grass (*Panicum virgatum*)	3 to 6 feet tall	Dry to moist soil	Full sun to partial shade	5-9	✓	✓	✓	Attractive to butterflies. Provides cover, food, and nesting material for ground-feeding and game birds.	Northeast, Southeast, Midwest, Southwest, partial West
Nuttall's Sunflower (*Helianthus nuttallii*)	3 to 8 feet tall	Moist to wet soil	Sun	5-9	✓			Blooms late summer through fall.	West, partial Southwest, partial Midwest

ALSO CONSIDER THE FOLLOWING NATIVE PLANTS IF YOU HAVE A DRY GARDEN AREA

Plant name	Plant size	Water needs	Preferred lighting conditions	Hardy to (USDA zones)	Provides			Main season of interest	Native range
					✿	⛰	⬡		
Wild Bergamot (*Monarda fistulosa*)	3 to 4 feet tall	Dry to moist, well-draining soil	Full sun to partial shade	3-8	✓			Lavender flowers from June through August that attract hummingbirds.	West
Big Sagebrush (*Artemisia tridentata*)	Up to 10 feet tall	Dry, rocky soil	Full sun	4-9		✓	✓	Evergreen shrub provides cover.	West
Virginia Strawberry (*Fragaria virginiana*)	6 inches	Dry to moist	Sun to shade	3-8	✓			Blooms April-June followed by fruits—works well as a groundcover.	Northeast, Southwest, West, Midwest
Smooth Aster (*Symphyotrichum laeve*)	Up to 3 feet tall	Dry, rocky soil	Full sun	4-8	✓			Flowers in fall and also attracts native bees and butterflies.	Midwest, partial Northeast, partial Southeast, Southwest, partial West
Western Juniper (*Juniperus occidentalis*)	15 to 50 feet tall	Dry, rocky soil	Full sun	5-9	✓	✓	✓	The cones attract Townsend's Solitaires, Clark's Nutcrackers, Cedar Waxwings, and American Robins.	West
Blue Grama (*Bouteloua gracilis*)	3 feet tall and wide	Dry, well-drained, gravely soil	Full sun	3-10	✓			Attracts seed-eating birds.	Midwest, Southwest
Whitebark Pine (*Pinus albicaulis*)	10 to 40 feet tall	Dry/drained soil	Sun	4-8	✓	✓		Fun fact: An ounce of Whitebark Pine seeds has more calories than chocolate. Also very resistant to wind.	West (mountains)
Pinyon Pine/Piñon Pine (*Pinus edulis*)	10 to 40 feet tall	Dry/drained soil	Sun	5-8	✓	✓		At least nine species of birds eat the seeds.	West (mountains)
Ponderosa Pine (*Pinus ponderosa*)	Up to 150 feet high	Dry to moist soil	Full sun to shade	3-8	✓	✓		Many animals and birds eat the seeds.	West, partial Midwest, partial Southwest

Red-Spike Mexican Hat (*Ratibida columnifera*) is a colorful native perennial to add to a mountain habitat garden.

Morgan Amos

📍 EAST CENTRAL WYOMING, ALONGSIDE THE NORTH PLATTE RIVER

While working in her vegetable garden, Morgan noticed movement near the garden hose that was set up for furrow-watering. Bathing in the stream of water flowing out of the hose was a little female Anna's Hummingbird.

"The encounter of watching her bathe opened my eyes to another side of bird life," she explained. "It was like, 'Wow, if I can put water out here that the birds will use, what else can I offer them?'" Days later, Morgan had hummingbird feeders, a birdbath, and a regular birdseed feeder set up to welcome more avian guests to her Bakersfield, California garden where the birds are year-round residents.

Today Morgan lives in a rural area of Wyoming, where western and eastern species of birds overlap on her property. Her backyard opens to woodland habitat, filled with lots of trees separated by lawn, which attracts many typical backyard birds, roosting Turkey Vultures and Wild Turkeys, a variety of thrushes, and some of the more common sparrows and warblers.

"We normally put out white proso millet for the Lazuli Buntings, that are nearly turquoise blue with creamy bellies and rusty breasts. One year, I found myself staring with amazement at one of their eastern counterparts—an all blue Indigo Bunting. We also have mostly Black-headed Grosbeaks from the west in our area, but occasionally, I will spot a most handsome Rose-breasted Grosbeak from the east," she said. One of the most noteworthy guests includes a hybrid Bullock's x Baltimore Oriole. "Bullock's Orioles are the western counterpart to the Baltimore Orioles and primarily what I get to see in my region, but this hybrid has visited my orange feeders for the past three springs, and exhibits characteristics of both species," she said.

Morgan Amos keeps a pair of binoculars on hand for quick viewing of the birds that visit her property.

Overlapping habitat areas bring through a variety of birds, especially during the migration season. "Behind our house is a more montane area, with plenty of junipers and Pinyon Pines. Occasionally birds like Pinyon Jays, nuthatches, and Mountain Chickadees will sweep down from higher elevations and visit my feeders."

Near Morgan's property are more agricultural fields and grassland areas, which include "all the larks (Meadowlarks, Horned Larks, Lark Buntings, and Lark Sparrows)." In addition to songbirds, the property also attracts waterfowl, shorebirds, and fish-eating raptors, due to the proximity to the river and a local pond. "My experience with birding has shown me the importance of wetland preservation and turning your yard into a habitat that can support some of our wildlife, rather than just a sterile patch of non-native lawn with a few imported, bug-and-disease-resistant bushes," she said.

Morgan offers resident birds food, water, and cover, with the main emphasis on multi-purpose plantings that double as food and cover. "We have only been in our current house for three years, but during that time, I have planted a few fruiting hedges, including two rows of American Elderberries, a row of Red Osier Dogwoods, half a dozen serviceberry shrubs, a hedge of American Cranberrybush Viburnums, and a handful of assorted fruit trees," she said.

Morgan shares her love of birds and the outdoors on social media, and her enthusiasm for birds spreads to visitors to her garden and her neighbors as well, who are surprised by the brightly colored, almost tropical-looking birds in the intermountain west. She's also able to point out nests of Great Horned Owls, Eastern Screech-Owls, Eastern Kingbirds, American Robins, House Wrens, and House Finches.

"There is nothing like watching the festival of feathers gathered around my feeding station on a cold and gloomy, otherwise miserable, day in February. In a world cloaked in deafening white, I can look out the window and see and hear the crowing of bright blue Pinyon Jays; American Goldfinches in their more muted, bronzy winter garb; the acrobatic moves of a yammering Red-breasted Nuthatch; and the chattering of shiny, tuxedo-clad Magpies. I admire them all, right down to my loyal and devoted House Finches and Dark-eyed Juncos."

A Pinyon Jay is a welcome sight.

PART IV

Conclusion

Y ou—as a gardener, bird enthusiast, bird watcher, bird feeder—play an important role in the conservation and success of the songbirds who gather in our gardens. Often making simple choices—such as avoiding pesticide use—can go a long way in making properties bird-friendly and sustainable for various bird populations. You do not need to have a large space, but the more "wild" area you can offer will be beneficial for the resident and migrating birds that will visit the garden.

Your garden—whether a balcony, front garden, container collection, or large back rural area—acts as an ambassador for other properties. Showing that native plants that support birds can be incorporated into foundation plantings in restricted areas, such as condo developments, help to start the conversation about what other native plants will meet the mark (there are lots). The projects in this book provide examples and jumping off points for you to experiment with your own property.

Birds need all the help they can get—and it starts with you. The State of the Birds report (2022) showed that a majority of bird populations are declining. One example that did well was waterfowl, because measures have been put in to place to help these populations. While bird conservation groups work to protect birds on a larger scale, your local planting area can make a difference today. Even plants that take a long time to reach maturity will provide benefits early on, such as oak trees when they are small, or native flowering perennials. As the plants age, they will fill in more, providing less area for weeds and invasives to take root. It won't be labor-less—plants in their first year need consistent watering to become established (even xeric varieties). Once established, the care for natives usually lessens, and you'll get to know the plant cycle.

Native plants can fit in with preexisting garden structures and design, such as this Spicebush (*Lindera benzoin*) in front of a greenhouse.

Gray Catbirds will be attracted to fruiting plants in the garden.

Also, be open to native plants that are classified as "weeds" by some, such as Pokeweed (*Phytolacca americana*) and Fleabane (*Erigeron annuus*), which provide food for birds.

You may begin with replacing one non-native plant with a native, or starting a garden by removing a small area of grass. Part of gardening for birds is being observant, and this applies to the garden and plants, too. Keeping an eye on when rainfall will be limited in the weather forecast and planning to provide supplemental watering can help first-year plantings. Paying attention to how much sun an area receives will help you choose a plant appropriate for the space.

Start small. Read books. Read bird websites. Learn about the birds through various programs, such as banding sessions during the migration seasons or resident birds who have become injured and can no longer survive in the wild. Learn bird facts. Share them with children.

By identifying birds—and the plants they need to survive—we can help turn the tide of bird and plant blindness that exists in society today. There are various ways to get started. Plant seeds. Buy small plants or shrubs. Plant a young tree, or if the budget allows, a larger slightly older variety. Leave leaves in an area of your garden for insects to hide in—and provide a spot for birds to rifle and hunt through.

We can normalize and make it apparent that certain birds need certain plants to eat or shrubs for cover. And creating habitats for the various birds has a beneficial effect on our wellness and welfare as well.

An American Robin on a birdbath.

Northern Mockingbird in Pokeweed (*Phytolacca americana*).

Resources

WEBSITE RESOURCES

The following websites provided information and resources about native plants.

The National Audubon Society. Plants for Birds. Native plants help support our birds throughout the year. www.audubon.org/PLANTSFORBIRDS

The National Audubon Society. Guide to North American Birds. www.audubon.org/bird-guide

The Lady Bird Johnson Wildflower Center—Plant Database. www.wildflower.org/plants/

California Native Plant Society—Calscape. calscape.org/

California Native Plant Society. www.cnps.org/

The Morton Arboretum—Search Trees and Plants. mortonarb.org/plant-and-protect/trees-and-plants/

The Cornell Lab of Ornithology—All About Birds Bird Guide. www.allaboutbirds.org/guide/

Missouri Botanical Garden—Plant Finder. www.missouribotanicalgarden.org/plantfinder/plantfindersearch.aspx

North Carolina Extension Gardener Plant Toolbox. www.plants.ces.ncsu.edu/

Arbor Day Foundation—Tree Database. shop.arborday.org/treeguide

Prairie Moon Nursery. www.prairiemoon.com

New Moon Nursery. www.newmoonnursery.com

American Beauties Native Plants. abnativeplants.com

Washington Native Plant Society. www.wnps.org/native-plant-directory

BOOKS/FURTHER READING

The following books contain a deeper dive into specific gardening regions, information about birds, and our environment.

Tallamy, D. *Bringing Nature Home: Updated and Expanded. How You Can Sustain Wildlife with Native Plants.* Timber Press. (2007)

Tallamy, D. *Nature's Best Hope. A New Approach to Conservation That Starts in Your Yard.* Timber Press. (2019)

Tallamy, D. *The Nature of Oaks. The Rich Ecology of Our Most Essential Native Trees.* Timber Press. (2021)

The Cornell Lab of Ornithology. *All About Birds Southwest.* Princeton University Press. (2022)

The Cornell Lab of Ornithology. *All About Birds Midwest: Midwest US and Canada.* Princeton University Press. (2022)

The National Audubon Society. *Birds of North America.* (2021)

Kress, Stephen W. *The Audubon Society Guide to Attracting Birds.* Charles Scribner's Sons. (1985)

Miller, George Oxford. *Native Plant Gardening for Birds, Bees & Butterflies: Southwest.* Adventure Publications. (2021)

Miller, George Oxford. *Native Plant Gardening for Birds, Bees & Butterflies: Southern California.* Adventure Publications. (2022)

Sibley, David Allen. *What it's like to be a bird.* Alfred A. Knopf. (2020)

Tate, Peter. *Flights of Fancy.* Delacorte Press. (2007)

Lake-Thom, Bobby. *Spirits of the Earth: A Guide to Native American Nature Symbols, Stories and Ceremonies.* Plume Book. (1997)

Shewey, John. *The Hummingbird Handbook: Everything you need to know about these fascinating birds.* Timber Press. (2021)

Roth, S. *Bird-by-Bird Gardening: The Ultimate Guide to Bringing in Your Favorite Birds—Year after Year.* Rodale. (2006)

Adams, G. *Birdscaping Your Garden: A Practical Guide to Backyard Birds and the Plants That Attract Them.* Rodale Press. (1998)

Adams, G. *Gardening for the Birds: How to create a bird-friendly backyard.* Timber Press. (2013)

McCargo, Heather and Fialkoff, A. *Native Trees for Northeast Landscapes.* Wild Seed Project. (2021)

Bannick, Paul. *The Owl and the Woodpecker. Encounters with America's Most Iconic Birds.* The Mountaineers Books. (2008)

Stark, Eileen M. *Real gardens grow natives. Design, plant & enjoy a healthy Northwest garden.* Skipstone. (2014)

Roth, Sally. *The Backyard Bird Feeder's Bible. The A-to-Z Guide to Feeders, Seed Mixes, Projects, and Treats.* Rodale. (2000)

Clausen, R. & Tepper, G. *Deer-Resistant Native Plants for the Northeast.* Timber Press. (2021)

Baicich, P., Barker, M. & Henderson, C. *Feeding Wild Birds in America. Culture, Commerce & Conservation.* Texas A&M University Press. (2015)

Daniels, J. *Native Plant Gardening for Birds, Bees & Butterflies: Upper Midwest.* Adventure Publications. (2020)

References/Citations

The National Audubon Society. https://www.audubon.org/

Green, Penelope. "Young Urban Birders, Open Your Hearts to the Treetops! The birds come, the birds go. All that changes is the pecking order." June 23, 2018. https://www.nytimes.com/2018/06/23/style/birds-are-cool.html Accessed July 26, 2022

Chillag, Amy. "Birdwatching for peace of mind and better health." September 25, 2019. https://www.cnn.com/2018/11/12/health/sw-birding-for-health/index.html

U.S. Department of the Interior Fish and Wildlife Service. "Quick Facts: From the 2016 National Survey of Fishing, Hunting, and Wildlife-Associated Recreation." January 2018. https://www.census.gov/content/dam/Census/library/visualizations/2016/demo/fhw16-qkfact.pdf

U.S. Department of the Interior, U.S. Fish and Wildlife Service, and U.S. Department of Commerce, U.S. Census Bureau. "2016 National Survey of Fishing, Hunting, and Wildlife-Associated Recreation." Revised October 2018. https://www.census.gov/content/dam/Census/library/publications/2018/demo/fhw16-nat.pdf page 88-89

United States Environmental Protection Agency. "Ecoregions of North America." 2022. https://www.epa.gov/eco-research/ecoregions-north-america Accessed July 25, 2022.

Loss, S., Will, T. & Marra, P. "The impact of free-ranging domestic cats on wildlife of the United States." *Nat Commun* 4, 1396 (2013). https://doi.org/10.1038/ncomms2380 Accessed July 4, 2022.

McDonald, J., Maclean, M., Evans, M. & Hodgson, D. "Reconciling actual and perceived rates of predation by domestic cats." *Ecology and Evolution,* Vol. 5, Issue 14 (2015). https://doi.org/10.1002/ece3.1553 Accessed July 4, 2022.

Stuart, Tessa. "How to Stop Cats from Killing Birds." January 29, 2015. https://www.audubon.org/news/how-stop-cats-killing-birds

Bonnington, C., Gaston, K., & Evans, K. "Fearing the feline: domestic cats reduce avian fecundity through trait-mediated indirect effects that increase nest predation by other species." *Journal of Applied Ecology*, 2013,50,15–24. Accessed July 4, 2022.

U.S. Fish & Wildlife Service. "Threats to Birds." 2017. https://www.fws.gov/library/collections/threats-birds

Adirondacks Forever Wild. "Trees of the Adirondacks: Paper Birch (*Betula papyrifera*)." https://wildadirondacks.org/trees-of-the-adirondacks-paper-birch-betula-papyrifera.html. Accessed February 7, 2023.

Wikipedia. "Black Birders Week." https://en.wikipedia.org/wiki/Black_Birders_Week

McFadden, M. "Brent Peterkin leads way into Birdland." June 3, 2022. https://www.newhavenindependent.org/article/black_birders_week

Birdability home page. https://www.birdability.org/

Swanson, R. "The golden-cheeked Warbler Returns. Audubon Texas." https://tx.audubon.org/news/golden-cheeked-warbler-returns

University of Minnesota Extension. "Building a rain garden." (2018) https://extension.umn.edu/landscape-design/rain-gardens#choose-plants-1778663 Accessed September 9, 2022.

Melinda Russell Design, PennState Extension. "Rain Garden—Biodiversity." December 10, 2012. https://extension.psu.edu/rain-garden-biodiversity Accessed Sept. 9, 2022.

University of Nebraska-Lincoln. "Institute of Agriculture and Natural Resources UNL Water. Rain gardens." https://water.unl.edu/article/stormwater-management/rain-gardens Accessed Sept. 9, 2022.

Wilson, H. "The History of Bird Feeding—II. Maine Birds." https://web.colby.edu/mainebirds/2016/02/05/the-history-of-bird-feeding-ii/ Accessed Sept. 23, 2022.

Kress, Steve. "11 Tips for Feeding Backyard Birds." https://www.audubon.org/news/11-tips-feeding-backyard-birds. Sept.27, 2011. Accessed Sept. 24, 2022.

Bird-Friendly Blooms. "Making it easier to find native plants in your community." https://pa.audubon.org/conservation/bird-friendly-blooms. Accessed Sept. 29, 2022.

Juniata Valley Audubon Society. "Shade-Grown Coffee." September 3, 2018. https://www.jvas.org/category/shade-grown-coffee/ Accessed Sept. 29, 2022.

The National Audubon Society. "Audubon for Kids: The Hummingbird Wing Beat Challenge." April 22, 2020. https://www.audubon.org/news/the-hummingbird-wing-beat-challenge

Greenspan, J. "How to go birding by tree." *The National Audubon Society.* July 29, 2016. https://www.audubon.org/news/how-go-birding-tree

Fritts, Rachel. "Avian Superhighways: The Four Flyways of North America." May 16, 2022. https://abcbirds.org/blog/north-american-bird-flyways/ Accessed Oct. 9, 2022.

The National Audubon Society. "The Bird Migration Explorer Lets You Interact With Nature's Most Amazing Feat." Fall 2022. https://www.audubon.org/magazine/fall-2022/the-bird-migration-explorer-lets-you-interact

The National Audubon Society Bird-Friendly Buildings: Making Our Built Environment Safer for Birds. https://www.audubon.org/bird-friendly-buildings

Haig, S.M., Murphy, S.P., Matthews, J.H. et al. Climate-Altered Wetlands Challenge Waterbird Use and Migratory Connectivity in Arid Landscapes. *Sci Rep* 9, 4666 (2019). https://doi.org/10.1038/s41598-019-41135-y

Oregon State University (2019). Climate change negatively affects waterbirds in the American West. https://extension.oregonstate.edu/news/climate-change-negatively-affects-waterbirds-american-west Accessed Oct. 5, 2022.

Miller, D., Thetford, M., Verlinde, C., and Campbell, G. Seaside Goldenrod, Solidago Sempervirens Fact Sheet. University of Florida. https://edis.ifas.ufl.edu/publication/SG185

University of Florida Gardening Solutions. Salt-tolerant plants. Last modified July 5, 2022. https://gardeningsolutions.ifas.ufl.edu/design/landscaping-for-specific-sites/salt-tolerant-plants.html

University of Marilyn Extension. "Ornamental and Native Grasses for the Landscape." Last modified February 15, 2023. https://extension.umd.edu/resource/ornamental-and-native-grasses-landscape

Wilson, C.R. Colorado State University Extension. Ornamental grasses. October 2011. https://extension.colostate.edu/topic-areas/yard-garden/ornamental-grasses-7-232/

Ornamental Grasses for the Midsouth Landscape. Mississippi State University Extension. http://extension.msstate.edu/publications/ornamental-grasses-for-the-midsouth-landscape

Morris, K. The National Turfgrass Initiative. https://citeseerx.ist.psu.edu/viewdoc/download?doi=10.1.1.507.9075&rep=rep1&type=pdf

Root, T. Ditching grass could help your backyard thrive. The Washington Post. June 30, 2021. https://www.washingtonpost.com/climate-solutions/2021/06/30/climate-friendly-backyard/

Menunkatuck Audubon Society. Choose Native Plants for Birds. https://menunkatuck.org/plants-for-sale

Hunt, B. Attracting Owls to Your Backyard: Safely, Responsibly, Ethically. https://www.owlresearchinstitute.org/attracting-owls-to-your-backyard

Cirino, E. Why You Should Keep Your Birdbath Clean. The National Audubon Society. September 20, 2016. https://www.audubon.org/news/why-you-should-keep-your-birdbath-clean

Winger BM, Weeks BC, Farnsworth A, Jones AW, Hennen M, Willard DE. 2019 Nocturnal flight-calling behaviour predicts vulnerability to artificial light in migratory birds. Proc. R. Soc. B 286: 20190364. http://dx.doi.org/10.1098/rspb.2019.0364

Fritts, R. These Seven Bird Species are Most Likely to Collide with Windows. American Bird Conservancy. March 16, 2022. https://abcbirds.org/blog/frequent-colliders/

American Bird Conservancy. Glass Collisions: Why Birds Hit Glass. https://abcbirds.org/glass-collisions/why-birds-hit-glass/

Pierce, R. Attracting Purple Martins to Your Property. University of Missouri Extension. April 2014. https://extension.missouri.edu/publications/g9428

Porter, D. How to Succeed as a Purple Martin Landlord. Birdwatching.com 2008. https://www.birdwatching.com/tips/purplemartin_landlord.html

Salman, David. Xeriscaping: 8 Steps To Plan and Care For a Low-Maintenance, Low-Water Garden. (2021) https://www.highcountrygardens.com/gardening/xeriscaping Accessed Oct. 31, 2022.

Stabley, Justin. What is xeriscaping? How you can turn your lawn into a sustainable oasis. Sept. 5, 2022. https://www.pbs.org/newshour/science/how-xeriscaping-offers-a-water-efficient-environmentally-friendly-alternative-to-lawns Accessed Oct. 31, 2022.

Sax, B. How Ravens Came to the Tower of London. April 20, 2007. Society and Animals 15 (2007) 269-283. https://www.animalsandsociety.org/wp-content/uploads/2016/04/sax.pdf

Hannemann, E. Fun facts about birds in pop culture. Dec.2, 2021. https://www.birdsandblooms.com/birding/pop-culture-bird-facts/

Danko, L. Rain Gardens—the Plants. December 12, 2014. https://extension.psu.edu/rain-gardens-the-plants

The Cornell Lab of Ornithology. Do Birds Store Food For The Winter? April 1, 2009. https://www.allaboutbirds.org/news/do-birds-store-food-for-the-winter

Brittingham, Margaret C. Attracting Hummingbirds: Learn about the many aspects of hummingbirds and how to attract them to your property. (November 8, 2007). Accessed September 9, 2022. https://extension.psu.edu/attracting-hummingbirds

Tangley, Laura. July 28, 2014. Breeding Bird Survey Takes Birders to the Streets. https://www.nwf.org/Home/Magazines/National-Wildlife/2014/AugSept/Animals/Chandler-Robbins

Klocke, C. The Urgency and Necessity for Greenways: Five Questions with Charles A. Flink. NC State University College of Design. Feb. 25, 2020. https://design.ncsu.edu/blog/2020/02/25/the-urgency-and-necessity-for-greenways/

Just Traveling. Notable Greenway & Trail Systems in the US. May 2017. https://www.justraveling.com/alternative-travel/us-greenway-trail-systems/

The National Audubon Society. Audubon's Guide to Ethical Bird Photography and Videography. https://www.audubon.org/node/61956

National Park Service. Tallgrass Prairie—A Complex Prairie Ecosystem. https://www.nps.gov/tapr/learn/nature/a-complex-prairie-ecosystem.htm

Forest Preserve District Will County. The Buzz. Five facts about America's once vast prairie. August 27, 2021. https://www.reconnectwithnature.org/news-events/the-buzz/five-facts-about-americas-prairies/

Smithsonian's National Zoo & Conservation Biology Institute. Neotropical Migrator Birds FAQs. https://nationalzoo.si.edu/migratory-birds/neotropical-migratory-bird-faqs

Smithsonian's National Zoo & Conservation Biology Institute. About Bird Friendly Coffee. https://nationalzoo.si.edu/migratory-birds/about-bird-friendly-coffee

Hammoud, R., Tognin, S., Burgess, L. et al. Smartphone-based ecological momentary assessment reveals mental health benefits of birdlife. Sci Rep 12, 17589 (2022). https://doi.org/10.1038/s41598-022-20207-6

Carpenter, T. Milkweed is for the birds...and the Butterflies and Bees. Pheasants Forever. August 10, 2017. https://www.pheasantsforever.org/BlogLanding/Blogs/Field-Notes/Milkweed-is-for-the-Birds-%E2%80%A6-and-Butterflies-and-Be.aspx

PictureThis—Plant Identifier App | Plant Identification Online. https://www.picturethisai.com/

Means, T. Why has it been raining so hard? How climate change is causing heavier downpours. Oct. 6, 2021. https://ideas.ted.com/why-climate-change-causes-heavy-rain-and-flooding/

United States Environmental Protection Agency. Climate Change Indicators: Heavy Precipitation. https://www.epa.gov/climate-indicators/climate-change-indicators-heavy-precipitation

Harp, R. D., & Horton, D. E. (2022). Observed changes in daily precipitation intensity in the United States. *Geophysical Research Letters*, 49, e2022GL099955. https://doi.org/10.1029/2022GL099955

Morris, A. It's raining harder in the U.S. Northwestern Now. October 11, 2022. https://news.northwestern.edu/stories/2022/10/its-raining-harder-in-the-u-s/

Cappucci, M. Study finds climate change is bringing more intense rains to U.S. October 11, 2022. https://www.washingtonpost.com/climate-environment/2022/10/11/rain-increasing-climate-change-us/

Illinois Extension. Gardening for climate change. February 11, 2019. https://extension.illinois.edu/blogs/flowers-fruits-and-frass/2019-02-11-gardening-climate-change

University of Wisconsin-Extension. Rain Gardens: A how-to manual for homeowners. https://dnr.wi.gov/topic/stormwater/documents/rgmanual.pdf

Iowa State University Extension and Outreach. Rain Gardens: Filtering and Recycling Rain Water. March 2013. https://store.extension.iastate.edu/product/Rain-Gardens-Filtering-and-Recycling-Rain-Water

Mark, J.J. Horus. World History Encyclopedia. March 16, 2016. https://www.worldhistory.org/Horus/

The National Audubon Society. Three Easy But Important Ways to Keep Your Bird Feeder Disease-Free. Dec. 6, 2010. https://www.audubon.org/news/three-easy-important-ways-keep-your-bird-feeder-disease-free

The National Audubon Society. Lights Out. https://www.audubon.org/lights-out-program

The National Audubon Society. Hummingbird Feeding FAQs. November 27, 2017. https://www.audubon.org/news/hummingbird-feeding-faqs

Bird Gap. 6 Kinds of Trees That Owls Like to Live in (Explained). June 11, 2022. https://birdgap.com/trees-owls-live/

Winston, T. A Guide to Luring Warblers, Tanagers, Orioles and Grosbeaks to Your Yard. The National Audubon Society. March 31, 2017. https://www.audubon.org/news/a-guide-luring-warblers-tanagers-orioles-and-grosbeaks-your-yard

The National Audubon Society. History of the Christmas Bird Count. https://www.audubon.org/conservation/science/christmas-bird-count/history-christmas-bird-count

Richie, M. Why Native Plants Are Better for Birds and People. The National Audubon Society. April 4, 2016. https://www.audubon.org/node/64191

Valenzuela, T. Bird migration and your yard. Sunday. June 1, 2021. https://www.getsunday.com/shed/backyard-living/wildlife/bird-migration-how-your-yard-can-help

Tallamy, Douglas W. March 11, 2015. "The Chickadee's Guide to Gardening." The New York Times. https://www.nytimes.com/2015/03/11/opinion/in-your-garden-choose-plants-that-help-the-environment.html

The National Audubon Society. Hummingbirds See Red. https://www.audubon.org/news/hummingbirds-see-red

The National Audubon Society. Climate Report. https://climate2014.audubon.org/all-species

USDA Hardiness Zones and Temps

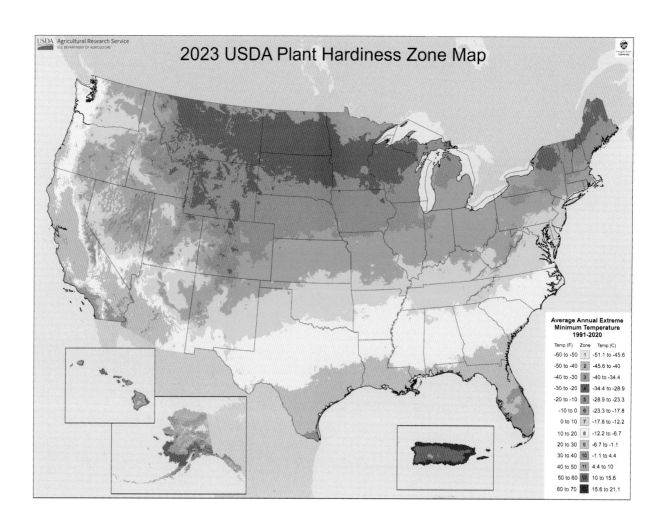

Photo Credits
A = All, B = Bottom, L = Left, M = Middle, R = Right, T = Top,

Agami Photo Agency/Shutterstock: 27B
Courtesy of Jamie Weiss: 84
Courtesy of Jason Kitting: 134
Courtesy of Jillian Bell: 94, 95
Courtesy of Laura Jackson: 158, 159
Courtesy of Morgan Amos: 176
Courtesy of Susie Creamer: 56, 57
Evan Barrientos/Audubon: 85
Illustrations by Mattie and Mike Wells: 62-63, 130-131, 148-149, 170-171
Jen McGuinness: 4, 6, 7,8 , 9, 10, 11, 12, 14, 15, 17, 20, 22, 23, 24L, 25, 26, 27T, 29, 30, 31, 32, 33, 34, 36, 39, 40, 41, 42, 43, 44, 45, 47, 48, 49, 50, 51, 52, 53, 58, 59, 61, 66, 67, 68, 69, 70, 71, 72, 73, 74, 76T, 77, 80, 81, 83, 86, 87, 89, 90, 91, 97, 99, 100T, 100M, 102, 103, 104, 105, 108, 109, 110, 114, 115, 116, 117, 120, 121, 122, 123, 129R, 133, 136, 137, 138, 139, 141, 142T, 142M, 143, 150, 152, 153, 154, 155, 157, 160, 161T, 161M, 164, 165, 167, 169L, 178, 179, 185
JLY Gardens: 75, 175
Judd Patterson Photography: 24R, 129L, 135, 146, 169R
Mia McPherson, On the Wing Photography: 76B, 100B, 140
Shutterstock: Kendall Collett, 37; Alison Hancock, 96; HeavilyMeditated, 142B; Chad Zuber, 161B; MelaniWright, 177
USDA: 184

Meet Jen McGuinness

Jen McGuinness is a writer, editor, photographer, and a life-long gardener.

She has been blogging as Frau Zinnie (FrauZinnie.com) since 2011, where she shares her own gardening experiences and interviews with gardening experts. She has been a guest on several gardening podcasts. Jen is the author of *Micro Food Gardening: Project Plans and Plants for Growing Fruits and Veggies in Tiny Spaces* (Cool Springs Press, 2021). She is a proponent of growing your own food using organic and pollinator-friendly methods and creating wildlife-friendly gardens. Her photos have been published in magazines and newspapers and she is an award-winning former journalist.

Author Acknowledgments

Songbirds have fascinated me since I was a child, but for a long time, I took their existence for granted. It was only as I evolved in my path as an organic gardener that I realized that the birds visiting the garden were not guaranteed, unless we all chipped in to help them exist. The idea for bird-friendly gardening as a book percolated for a few years and I'm grateful I was able to partner with The Quarto Group to create the book in your hands.

Thank you to the team at The Quarto Group/ Cool Springs Press, especially my editor Jessica Walliser, for seeing the value in this topic and championing the cause. Many thanks to Regina Grenier, Brooke Pelletier, Mattie Wells, Michael Wells and Anne Van Nest, along with the many other members of the Quarto editing and design team who contributed to making a written manuscript into the beautiful book in your hands.

Thank you to Laura Jackson, Jillian Bell, Susie Creamer, Morgan Amos, Jason Kitting, Jamie Weiss, and Evan Barrientos who enthusiastically shared their personal experiences and photos for the profiles in this book. Thank you to Ola Rucz for sharing your talent and artwork and Jen Ott for keeping it real. Thank you to Angie Lituri, Amy Jahnke, Kelle Young, Amanda Foley and Michelle Engel for sharing your time and gardens, and of course, friendship. Thank you to all of the experts at the National Audubon Society who contributed their avian knowledge: Betty Su, Julisa Colón, Holly Fairall, Jennifer Bogo, Kristina Deckert, Sabine Meyer, Melanie Ryan, Camilla Cerea, Dr. Chad Wilsey, Geoff LeBaron, Chad Witko, Marlene Pantin and Connie Sanchez.

Thanks to Bob and Del McGuinness for opening your garden for my native plant visions, and to Ginny Werblow and Nancy Mueller for generously opening your garden for photographs of native trees and shrubs. And of course, thank you to my husband, Rob, for your unconditional support and love, for entertaining my gardening ideas and believing in me.

Index